REMAINS

Historical and Literary

CONNECTED WITH THE PALATINE COUNTIES OF

Lancaster and Chester

VOLUME XX—THIRD SERIES

MANCHESTER:

Printed for the Chetham Society

1972

IN MEMORY OF E. F. JACOB

Professor Ernest Fraser Jacob, the President of the Society, died in All Souls College, Oxford, on October 7th, 1971, aged 77, and all of our members who knew him personally can only have been profoundly saddened by the news. He had long been a true friend of the Society: joining it in 1933 when he also became a member of Council, in 1938 he succeeded the late Col. John Parker as President, an office he was prevailed upon to retain until his death, his tenure being only ever surpassed in length by that of James Crossley, the Society's 'founder' and second President (1847–83). Dr. Jacob, Professor of Medieval History in the University of Manchester since 1929, returned to Oxford in 1944, subsequently (1950) being elected to the Chichele Chair of Modern History from which he retired in 1961, continuing to the very end, however, his active interest in scholarly work and literary production. But although E. F. J. lived away from Manchester for by far the greater part of the period of his Presidency, he was never out of touch with affairs at headquarters. Indeed, he constantly maintained a direct interest in proposals for publication, 'vetted' manuscripts with the careful help of his Vice-President, Dr. G. H. Tupling, until the latter's death in 1962, and until not far short of his last illness presided, whenever possible, at the annual meetings of the Council and of the members (on the last occasion flying up from Heathrow in order to do so). Dr. Tupling had been elected as Vice-President when Professor Jacob became President, and together they made an ideal pair of co-directors: the former brought the detailed knowledge and expertise of the practising local historian of the region, the President a warm appreciation of the significance of local history as an integral part of the national story and the 'statesmanship' and vision of the historian of great reputation with important interests and connexions in the wider world outside. E. F. J. was the beneficent *seigneur*, G. H. T. his mild-mannered, efficient seneschal of the lordship. The partnership was entirely salutary, and our late President had every reason to be satisfied with the Society's development under his guidance. In 1938 its membership stood at 185 (69 private members); by 1971 it has risen to 266 (83). Its publications during that time have maintained a roughly even balance between records and works of the monograph type and between the claims to consideration of the two palatine counties constituting the Society's sphere of interest. And they numbered thirty all told: a remarkable record considering the disruptions of the war-years, not to mention the constraints imposed ever since by constantly rising printing costs. It may confidently be said, without complacency, that our late President left his Society in good shape. The members of the Council wish to record their deep sense of gratitude for all the good work he did for it.

The
LANCASHIRE TEXTILE
INDUSTRY
in the
SIXTEENTH CENTURY

by
Norman Lowe

MANCHESTER
Printed for the Chetham Society
1972

© 1972 The Chetham Society

Published for the Society by
Manchester University Press
316–324 Oxford Road
Manchester M13 9NR

ISBN 0 7190 1156 6

Printed in Great Britain by Butler & Tanner Ltd., Frome and London

CONTENTS

LIST OF TABLES

ABBREVIATIONS

Bowden

P. J. Bowden, *The Wool Trade in Tudor and Stuart England*
London, 1962.

C.C.R.

Court Rolls of the Honour of Clitheroe.
3 vols., ed. W. Farrer,
Manchester, 1897, 1912 and 1913.

Econ. H.R.

Economic History Review.

E.H.R.

English Historical Review.

S.P.D.

State Papers, Domestic.

V.C.H.L.

Victoria County History of Lancs.

Wadsworth and Mann

A. P. Wadsworth & J. de L. Mann,
The Cotton Trade and Industrial Lancashire,
1600–1780.
Manchester, 1931, repr. 1965.

The publication of this volume
has been aided by
a generous grant from
the Pasold Research Fund
for which the Council
of the Society is grateful

CHAPTER 1

LANCASHIRE AND LANCASHIRE CLOTH
IN THE SIXTEENTH CENTURY

BEFORE it was scarred by the Industrial Revolution, Lancashire must have presented an attractive face. Almost the whole of the eastern part of the county consists of uplands which form a section of the Pennine Chain. This is still fine, wild and bleak moorland, often heather-covered in the south, and with magnificent hills rising to strange, flat, slab-like summits such as Blackstone Edge, Pendle Hill and Boulsworth Moor. In the deep valleys between these summits and sometimes on the slopes of the moors themselves, there were small market towns and villages: Bolton, Bury, Oldham, Rochdale, Blackburn, Accrington, Clayton-le-Moors, Padiham, Burnley and Colne, where textiles were made in the cottages. Between these settlements there was only a thin scattering of hamlets and farms.

Towards the west the moors descend into the fertile, rolling, lowland country of the coastal plain. Here, almost on the estuary of the River Ribble, stood the ancient town of Preston, a free borough since Henry II had granted the burgesses a gild merchant in a charter of 1197.[1] Further south was Wigan, another corporate town. From this southern Lancashire coastal area the plain reaches far eastwards around the valley of the River Mersey, and it was on this central southern plain that Manchester and Salford, the two most important centres of textile manufacture, grew up.

John Leland, on his travels around England, passed through Lancashire in 1535 and had this to write about what he saw:[2]

I rode over Mersey water by a great bridge of tymbre caullid Crosford Bridge. This water of Mersey to the veri maine se departith Chestreshire and Lancastreshire. So about a iii. miles to Manchestre. . . . Mancestre on the south side of Irwel River stondith in Salfordshiret, and is the fairest, best buildid, quikkest, and most populus tounne of al Lancastreshire; yet is in hit but one paroch chirch, but is a college. . . . Ther be divers stone bridgis in the toune, but the best of iii. arches is over Irwel, cawllid Salford Bridge. This bridge devidith Manchester from Salford, the wich is as a large suburbe to Manchester. On this bridge is a

---

[1] H. Fishwick, *History of the Parish of Preston*, p. 13.
[2] J. Leland, *Itinerary*, iv, pp. 5–6.

praty litle chapel. The next is the bridge that is over Hirke river, on the wich the fair builded college standith.

The ruins of 'Old Man Castel' were still to be seen just outside the town, but its dilapidation had been hastened on by the fact that stones from the ruins 'wer translatid toward making of bridgges for the toune'.[1] On the Irk were 'divers fair milles that serve the toune'. The actual area covered by the town itself was quite small. The main buildings—the church with its college and the toll-booth or town-hall—were clustered together and formed the town centre, along with Manchester market place, on the south side of the church. The pillory and stocks probably stood in the market place, which was surrounded by the houses and shops of some of the traders.[2] Two roads led into the town—Deansgate from the south and Millgate from the north—both lined with houses, and joined in the centre of the town by other streets with picturesque names like Hanging Ditch, St. Mary's Gate, and Market Sted Lane where the conduit stood from which the town drew its water supply.[3] William Camden who paid a visit in 1585, agreed with Leland, and considered that Manchester surpassed all the neighbouring towns in the quality of its buildings and in size of population,[4] which was probably somewhere in the region of two thousand at the time of the Armada.[5]

There was no doubt in the minds of contemporaries about where Manchester's claim to fame lay. By 1541 cloth manufacture had grown so important that the sanctuary had to be moved to Chester because it had been attracting 'divers light and evill disposed persons' to Manchester who had acquired the disturbing habit of stealing linen yarn as it lay outside bleaching and woollen cloth as it hung on the tenterhooks drying. The preamble to the Act states that the 'Towne of Manchestre is and hath of long tyme ben a towne well inhabited . . . and the Inhabitants of the same towne well sett a worke in making of Clothes, as well of lynnen as of wollen'.[6] Camden was much impressed and wrote: 'it has the best trade of any in these Northern parts . . . Manchester surpasses the towns here-abouts in Woollen manufacture . . . woollen cloths call'd Manchester cottons'.[7]

---

[1] J. Leland, *Itinerary*, iv, p. 6.

[2] *Victoria County History of Lancaster*, iv, p. 176 passim.

[3] *Manchester Court Leet Records*, i, p. 15, ed. J. P. Earwaker.

[4] W. Camden, *Britannia*, ii, p. 962.

[5] In 1588 Manchester town and parish were required to supply two hundred and eighty men for military service. (J. Aston, *Picture of Manchester*, p. 14.) If one assumes that only half the adult males were fit for service, this would give a total of say 500 adult males. Multiplied by 4, this gives the figure of 2000 for the total population. A similar calculation was suggested by E. E. Rich to estimate the population of England at this time. (*Economic H.R.*, Second Series, vol. II, 1949/50.) This tallies quite well with a somewhat vague estimate made about 1711 that at the time of the Civil War the population of town and parish was '2000, 3000 or 4000'. This is quoted by Wadsworth and Mann, p. 509.

[6] 33 Henry VIII, cap. 15.   [7] Camden, op. cit., ii, p. 963.

Leland passed on to visit Bolton and Bury and noted: 'Bolton apon Moore market stondith most by cottons and cowrse yarne. Divers villages in the mores abowt Bolton do make cottons.'[1] Bury did not impress him quite so much. 'Yerne sometime made abowte Byri a market towne on Irwel . . . 4 or v miles from Manchestre, but a poore market.'[2] Rochdale, which lay on a Roman road leading over Blackstone Edge into Yorkshire, was more striking and had the distinction of possessing a grammar school founded in 1562 at a time when there were only about half a dozen in the whole county.[3] Rochdale market, in the words of Camden, was 'of no small resort'.[4]

Preston was a centre of both linen and woollen manufacture and in 1535 Leland commented that its market place was fair.[5] By 1562 there had been a great increase since the beginning of the century in the number of weavers and flax sellers shown on the burgess roll.[6] Camden thought the town 'large, handsome and populous, for these partes'.[7] William Banestre, the Mayor in 1571, reported that the most common type of cloth made in Preston was narrow white kerseys.[8]

Unfortunately neither Camden nor Leland visited the other Lancashire centres. Practically nothing seems to have been discovered about Blackburn in the sixteenth century, but more is known about Burnley. This was nothing more than a tiny hamlet on the banks of the river Brun in 1400, but during the sixteenth century it expanded rapidly and by 1550 the population of the parish may well have been approaching twelve hundred.[9] There had been a fulling mill in the village before 1300; by 1600 the market place, where the Tuesday market had been held for over three hundred years, was surrounded by shops and by work rooms housing mainly weavers.[10] Colne seems to have been a flourishing township in the sixteenth century. It consisted of one main street climbing gently up a hillside, and on the top of the hill, the parish church which was almost completely rebuilt about 1515. As well as Colne the parish included the hamlets of Foulridge, Marsden, Trawden and Barrowford, containing altogether about four hundred households with a population of some fifteen hundred.[11]

It was in these places and in the surrounding countryside that the cloth was manufactured. But what of the cloth itself; what type of cloth was it? There were four main sorts of woollen cloth manufactured: rugs, friezes, kerseys, and cottons. All of them were narrow cloths produced on a narrow

[1] Leland, op. cit., v, p. 43.
[2] ibid., v, p. 43.
[3] H. Fishwick, *History of the Parish of Rochdale*, p. 270.
[4] ibid., p. 39.
[5] Leland, op. cit., iv, p. 9.
[6] H. Fishwick, *History of Preston*, p. 46.
[7] ibid., p. 48.
[8] D.L.1/83, L.26.
[9] W. Bennett, *History of Burnley, 1400–1650*, p. 37.
[10] ibid., pp. 44, 77–8.
[11] W. Bennett, *History of Marsden and Nelson*, p. 78.

loom, operated by one man (as opposed to broadcloth which was made on a broad loom requiring two men to operate it). The first two types were apparently very similar in character, a rather coarse cloth which, according to the Act of 1551,[1] was expected to be thirty-six yards long and three quarters of a yard wide. They appear to have been usually white, grey or black, although 'tawney' coloured friezes were sometimes produced. They were made chiefly in the Manchester area, in Bury, Bolton, and in Rochdale. Kerseys were a much shorter cloth, only eighteen yards long and one yard wide, and also lighter in weight than rugs and friezes. They were manufactured mostly in the north-eastern part of the county in Colne, Burnley, Padiham and Blackburn, and also in Preston. The fourth type of cloth, cottons, presents something of a problem because there has been some dispute over the exact nature of the cloth, whether cottons were really woollen cloth at all. If one relies on the views of contemporary writers, then there can be no doubt that Manchester cottons consisted purely and simply of wool. Camden was perfectly clear on the point: 'woollen cloths call'd Manchester cottons', he wrote.[2] The statutes passed to regulate the manufacture of cloth in the sixteenth century, and which refer to Manchester and Lancashire cottons as well as to other types of cottons, leave no doubt from their titles and wording that they are meant to deal with woollen cloth.[3]

One of the earliest writers about the cotton industry, Andrew Ure, did not question the fact that Manchester cottons were a type of woollen.[4] Yet when the Victoria County History of Lancashire appeared in 1908 the authors seemed to have confused 'cottons' with 'fustians' and assumed that cottons were only half woollen, and contained a linen warp.[5] There is no evidence whatsoever to support this theory but unfortunately it has since been stated as fact by more than one writer.[6] Professor G. W. Daniels writing later, put forward a different idea.[7] 'While it can definitely be stated that cottons were regarded as woollen goods in the sixteenth century,' he wrote, 'it is hard to resist a suspicion that the vegetable fibre, cotton, may have been used in the manufacture of Lancashire cloths. The fact that they were regarded as woollens is not of itself conclusive, as, at that time, cotton was usually called cotton-wool. Further, there is the circumstance of their comparatively light weight.'

Again, however, the theory seems doubtful. If cottons had contained

[1] 5 and 6 Edward VI, cap. 6.

[2] Camden, op. cit., ii, p. 963.

[3] 5 and 6 Edward VI, cap. 6, and 4 and 5 Philip and Mary, cap. 5, for instance.

[4] A. Ure, *Cotton Manufacture of Great Britain Investigated and Illustrated*, i, p. 100.

[5] *V.C.H.L.*, ii, p. 296.

[6] For example, by A. K. Longfield, *Anglo-Irish Trade in the Sixteenth Century*, p. 156, and as recently as 1950 by A. L. Rowse, *The England of Elizabeth*, p. 147.

[7] G. W. Daniels, *Early English Cotton Industry*, pp. 7–8. Also by B. Hewart, *Economic Journal*, x, 1910, p. 24.

some real cotton, clothiers would presumably have kept a stock of cotton along with their wool. But in no case was a weaver discovered who owned cotton, or cotton-wool, or any other commodity which might be suspected of having been cotton. Men who made inventories were usually most painstaking about the different items, and often took the trouble to distinguish even between the different types of wool. They would not be likely to miss repeatedly a novelty like the 'Bombast or Downe . . . commonly called cotton wooll'.[1] Yet John Broxopp, a typical Blackburn 'cottonman', had among his raw materials no cotton or cotton-wool; there was no flax or linen yarn either; simply thirty-five stones of wool.[2]

Nor is the fact about their 'comparative lightness' at all conclusive. Although it is true that cottons were lighter than rugs and friezes, they were in fact, slightly heavier than kerseys,[3] and there is no question of kerseys containing anything other than wool. Consequently there can be little doubt that cottons consisted solely of wool. This was the conclusion reached by Wadsworth and Mann[4] and echoed by Mendenhall[5] who, when writing of Welsh cottons which were similar in weight to their Lancashire counterpart, claimed that they were a coarse woollen material whose nap was raised with teasels, or cottoned, a process which gave it a softer fluffy appearance like that of real cotton. These cloths which were produced in a variety of different colours, were manufactured in the Manchester area, in Bolton and Bury, and in the district around Blackburn.

So much for Lancashire woollens; but there was another type of cloth produced about which very little has been written anywhere, at least concerning its manufacture in the sixteenth century. This was linen, which seems to have been woven almost everywhere in the county, except in those districts such as Colne and Rochdale, bordering on the West Riding of Yorkshire. Manchester, Wigan, Preston, Ormskirk and Blackburn were all important centres of linen production.

Table 1. The comparative weights of Lancashire cloth (based on the statistics laid down by the Act of 1551, 5 and 6 Edward VI, cap. 6).

Type of cloth	length in yards	width in yards	weight in pounds	approx. weight in oz. sq. yd.
rugs and friezes	36	¾	48	28·4
kerseys	18	1	20	17·8
cottons (Manchester and Lancashire)	33 (22 goads)	¾	30	19·4
cottons (Welsh)	48 (32 goads)	¾	46	20·4

---

[1] So described in a petition of the London fustian dealers to Parliament in 1621. Quoted by Wadsworth and Mann, p. 15.

[2] Inventory of John Broxopp, 1582/3.

[3] See table 1.   [4] pp. 16–17.

[5] T. C. Mendenhall, *Shrewsbury Drapers and the Welsh Wool Trade*, p. 4.

CHAPTER II

SOURCES OF RAW MATERIAL

THE healthy existence of any industry depends on a plentiful supply of raw materials. The Lancashire linen and woollen industries were fortunate in having supplies of flax, hemp, and raw wool near at hand. Flax and hemp were both grown in west Lancashire on the estates of the wealthy Shuttleworth family at Hoole, near Preston. Their accounts are scattered with items such as: 'xv weemen which pulled flaxe a day at Hoole, for the tablynge of the said weemen onne daye iiij^s iij^d; for table ale iiij^d.'[1] 'John wiffe Mosse for pullinge hemp and layinge it in wite and dryinge it againe ij^s.'[2]

The coastal districts produced their share of raw materials; in 1503 Lytham Priory was receiving tithes paid in flax and hemp[3] and the same happened at Poulton and at St. Michael's-on-Wyre in 1535.[4] Some thirty miles south of Preston was another centre of linen manufacture—Wigan, and again the tithe accounts show that flax and hemp were grown in the area.[5]

Elsewhere in the county there was some small-scale growing of flax—Whalley Abbey in the north-east collected tithes in flax in 1536 from the parishes of Whalley, Clitheroe and Downham, but their value was only small, no more than £1 12s.[6] Even Manchester, whose soil one might have expected to be unsuitable, nevertheless managed to produce some raw materials for its linen industry, according to the Charter of Foundation given by Elizabeth to Manchester College in 1587.[7] The Charter reveals that the Warden and Fellows of the College were to be given all the tithes of flax, hemp, and wool in the parish.

[1] *Shuttleworth Accounts*, i, p. 53; ed. J. Harland.

[2] ibid., p. 100.

[3] H. Fishwick, *The History of the Parish of Lytham*, p. 90. Chetham Society, New Series, vol. 60, 1907.

[4] H. Fishwick, *The History of the Parish of Poulton-le-Fylde*, pp. 41–3; and *The History of the Parish of St. Michael's on Wyre*, p. 45. Chetham Society, New Series, vol. 8, 1885; and vol. 25, 1891.

[5] G. T. O. Bridgeman, *History of the Church and Manor of Wigan*, i, pp. 101, 107, 125, 127. Chetham Society, New Series, vol. 15, 1888.

[6] *Clitheroe Court Rolls*, iii, pp. 408–12; ed. W. Farrer.

[7] *Manchester Court Leet Records*, i, p. 100; ed. J. Harland.

Locally grown flax and hemp supplied only a minute percentage of the linen industry's needs, however. The Shuttleworths, for instance, although they grew flax and hemp on their estates, still required extra supplies which they bought at Manchester.[1] William Hodgkinson, a Preston merchant, had a hundred bales of flax brought from London to Preston in 1564.[2] He came to an agreement with Robert Blackledge, a London merchant tailor who was in Preston at the time, that Blackledge should deliver the flax within two months, when the Preston man would pay him the sum of £21 14s. 10d. As security Hodgkinson presented Blackledge with a golden half angel, worth five shillings. In actual fact, it seems that the bulk of the raw materials for manufacturing Lancashire linens was drawn from Ireland.

As far as sources of raw wool are concerned, it is clear that the Lancashire woollen industry was better served by local supplies than the linen industry was. Lancashire clothiers probably relied quite heavily on wool produced in the northern counties. Clothiers in north and east Lancashire drew some of their supplies from the neighbouring West Riding of Yorkshire. In 1526, for instance, two Lancashire clothiers were in Halifax, where they bought thirty stones of wool from a Halifax clothier, John Hardy. The price was £10, and they agreed to pay within one month.[3] Apparently it was a common practice for Halifax clothiers to sell coarse Yorkshire wool to Rochdale clothiers, because they themselves preferred to use finer wool from Lincolnshire for their narrow kersies.[4]

There is a great deal of evidence to suggest that there were plentiful supplies of wool even closer at hand, produced in Lancashire itself. The whole of the north-eastern part of the county around the great Pendle Hill, where the market towns of Colne, Clitheroe and Burnley, and the Abbey of Whalley were situated, contained large numbers of sheep. As early as 1507 Richard Kendal was fined at Clitheroe for overstocking the common pasture with sixty sheep.[5] Two women each had sixty sheep on the common pasture at Haslingden, sixteen miles south-east of Burnley, in 1509. Both were called before the Halmote Court and fined 8d. each for their offence.[6] This was a regular occurrence during the early years of the century: in 1540 the Clitheroe Halmote Court fined four men for the same offence with a total of a hundred and seventy sheep.[7] In Burnley in 1532, three men were fined for having taken the unpardonable liberty of washing their sheep in the Cowhey at Roughlee, thus breaking a bye-law.[8]

Until the 1530's cattle had been more numerous than any other kind of stock raised in the Rossendale Valley, but by then sheep were becoming

[1] *Shuttleworth Accounts*, i, p. 55.
[2] D.L.1/62, B.17.   [3] C.1/639/43.
[4] *Historical MSS. Commission, Kenyon MSS*, p. 573.
[5] *C.C.R.* i, p. 24.   [6] ibid., iii, p. 15.   [7] ibid., i, p. 125.
[8] ibid., i, p. 107.

B

serious rivals. There are frequent mentions in the Clitheroe Court Rolls of sheep gates on both common and private pastures.[1] One comes across tenants in Wolfenden Booth and Bacup buying or taking on lease holdings with as many as thirty sheep gates on the commons.[2]

The Abbot of Whalley accepted payment of tithes in kind until the dissolution of the Abbey in 1537. He received large numbers of sheep and far from negligible amounts of wool from Whalley and from the ten other chapelries which lay under the Abbot's jurisdiction. In 1536, for example, the Abbey received two hundred and forty-five lambs valued at £15 11s. 8d., and a hundred and seven stones of wool valued at over £20.[3]

Table 2. Tithes of sheep, wool and flax received at Whalley Abbey in 1536.

Chapelry	Lambs	£ s. d.	Stones of wool	£ s. d.	Flax £ s. d.
Whalley	47 worth	2 7 0	10 worth	2 0 0	12 0
Clitheroe	16	16 0	4	16 0	13 4
Downham	16	16 8	6	1 4 0	6 8
Colne	10	10 0	11	2 2 0	
Burnley	24	4 0 0	18	5 10 0	
Church	40	2 0 0	12	2 8 0	
Haslingden	30	1 10 0	8	1 12 0	
Bowland	2	12 0	4	16 0	
Pendle	10	10 0	12	2 6 8	
Trawden	10	10 0	10	1 16 0	
Rossendale	40	2 0 0	12	2 8 0	
	245	15 11 8	107	22 18 8	1 12 0

If one assumes that these figures do, in fact, represent one tenth of all the lambs born and all the wool produced in the Abbot's area in 1536, one can form some notion of the rather modest quantities of raw materials which this small north-eastern corner of the county yielded during the first half of the sixteenth century.

Later in the century the situation was similar. A Colne clothier, Lawrence Blakey, who died in 1573, left somewhere in the region of a hundred sheep.[4] Nicholas Baldwin, also of Colne, owned sixty sheep valued at £6 when he died in 1583. A yeoman farmer of Tockholes, Blackburn, Thomas Baron, died in 1595 leaving sheep worth £14, numbering at least a hundred and ten, while William Bolton of Little Harwood, a contemporary of Baron, had at least eighty sheep valued at £10.[5]

[1] G. H. Tupling, *The Economic History of Rossendale*, p. 165.
[2] *C.C.R.*, iii, pp. 174–5.   [3] ibid., iii, pp. 408–12.
[4] See Appendix, p. 171; Will and inventory of Lawrence Blakey, 1573.
[5] Will and inventory of Nicholas Baldwin, 1583; Thomas Baron, 1595; William Bolton, 1594/5.

Probably one of the largest sheep owners in the district were the Shuttleworths, who had estates at Gawthorpe and Smithills, near Burnley, as well as at Hoole. It was on the Burnley estates that they kept sheep which in 1590 must have numbered between a thousand and fifteen hundred, judging from the amounts of wool they yielded during a year.[1] Local people could earn a few extra pence, as well as food and drink while they worked, by helping to clip the Shuttleworth sheep. Their farm accounts mention items such as:

Nicholas Pendleburie and his wyffe for clyppinge of shipe iiij d.
Unto uxor Tourner and hir folkes for wyasshinge and clyppinge of shippe vj d.
Nicholas Whitteney and Henry Walker sonne for helpinge to servffe the clyppeeres ij d.

Another entry for the same month, June 1586, was: 'For tene pound of piche for to marke shipe ij s.vj d.'[2]

Whatever had remained over after the Shuttleworths' own needs had been satisfied, was sold to local cloth producers in widely varying quantities. On one occasion in 1589 the receipts mention 6s. 9d. 'for towe stone of wolle wantinge a pounde and a halfe'.[3] Usually, however, a single buyer took not less than ten stones. In 1590 James Sudall bought fifty stones of wool for £25. Altogether in that year the Shuttleworths sold two hundred and sixteen stones, for which they received £108. The price was invariably 10s. a stone.[4] Five years later the price had increased to 13s. 4d. a stone, though in that year only ninety-nine stones of wool were sold.[5]

Another well-to-do family who reared sheep on their estates was the Stanleys, of Hornby Castle, near Lancaster. Their accounts for 1581/2 show them selling wool in Bolton where at one point ten and a half stones were sold at 8s. 6d. a stone.[6]

In the more southerly districts of the county towards Manchester, the situation was similar. The Rochdale Court Rolls show that as early as the fourteenth century, woollen cloth was being made from Rochdale grown wool.[7] It was quite common for small farmers or husbandmen to keep up to a hundred sheep. In 1540 no fewer than twelve men were fined at Tottington Halmote, near Bury, for overstocking the common pasture with numbers of sheep ranging from ten to eighty.[8] In fact on one day alone there were two hundred and thirty sheep pastured on the commons without

---

[1] According to Bowden, p. 37, the sheep of Lancashire and Yorkshire could produce a fleece weighing from 2 to 3 lb. The Shuttleworth sheep produced at least 216 stones in 1590.

[2] *Shuttleworth Accounts*, i, p. 28.   [3] *Shuttleworth Accounts*, i, p. 93.

[4] ibid., i, p. 94.   [5] ibid., i, p. 118.

[6] *Hornby Castle Accounts*, Chetham Society, New Series, vol. 102, 1939, pp. 97–8; ed. W. H. Chippindall.

[7] A. P. Wadsworth, *History of Rochdale Woollen Trade*, p. 90.

[8] *C.C.R.*, iii, p. 328.

a licence.[1] During the later part of the century Bury farmers continued to keep sheep and several of them[2] left inventories which mention between sixty and a hundred sheep, together with amounts of wool; a typical example is John Hardman who left seventy-seven sheep when he died in 1581.

In the Manchester area itself the typical sheep owner seems to have been rather more modest. I have found the inventories of a number of farmers[3] living in hamlets such as Eccles and Barton, who owned usually about thirty sheep each; but no-one seems to have kept substantially more than this.

This Lancashire wool, like that produced in Yorkshire, was not of a very high quality, being both short and coarse; each fleece would probably weigh between two and three pounds.[4] Nevertheless it was not the coarsest wool produced in England; the sheep of the border country—Cumberland and Northumberland—have the distinction of producing the poorest quality wool in the sixteenth and seventeenth century, while the finest quality came from Herefordshire, Shropshire and Staffordshire, where a fleece, being so fine, would usually weigh no more than one pound.[5]

Locally grown wool and Yorkshire wool did not satisfy all the demands of the Lancashire woollen producers. Some additional supplies of coarse wool were drawn into Lancashire from the Midlands.[6] A further source of wool for workers in the Manchester area was Ireland, which became increasingly important as the century progressed, as a source of both wool and linen yarn.

The history of the trade in raw wool and linen yarn between Ireland and England is somewhat complex, since it was subject to interference from both the Irish and English governments, each of which was concerned to safeguard, among other things, the interests of its subjects. The woollen trade was the first to suffer, when in 1522 the Irish Parliament passed an Act which completely prohibited the export of wool—'the lading of wooll and flockes out of this lande'.[7] Their intention was to safeguard the native Irish woollen industry which would naturally suffer if its life-blood continued to drain away to England. Not until 1569 did the Irish Parliament relent and remove the total prohibition. Even then almost equally prohibitive customs duties were placed on exported wool, and remained in force throughout the century.

The fact that quantities of wool did find their way from Ireland can be explained partly by the existence of smuggling and partly by the fact that

---

[1] *C.C.R.*, iii., p. 328.

[2] John Hardman, William Fletcher, (1602); John Lomax, (1605).

[3] John Derbeshire, (1592); Thomas Pollitt, (1588); Robert Ravald, (1578); John Riding, (1601).

[4] Bowden, p. 37.   [5] ibid, p. 29.

[6] Wadsworth, op. cit., p. 91.

[7] Longfield, op. cit., pp. 77–8.

the English Crown was in the habit of granting licences to favoured people, allowing the prohibition to be evaded. In 1534 for instance, Henry VIII granted John Travers, who was a gentleman waiter to the Duke of Richmond, a licence which stated that during the next seven years, he could send thirty-three sacks of Irish wool, each containing twenty-six stones and one pound to Chester, Liverpool or Bristol.[1] The following year John Forster was licensed to export to England two hundred stones of wool annually for six years.[2] Even when all licences were cancelled in 1537, one was allowed to stand, which permitted Edward Abecke of Manchester to take £40 worth of wool and flocks to England every year.[3]

Until 1569 the Irish had only been concerned with wool, and there had been no interference with the export of linen yarn from Ireland. But in that year the Irish government became seriously alarmed at the increasingly large amounts of linen yarn being sent to England, to the detriment of the home industry. An impossibly high tariff of a shilling was placed on every pound of linen yarn and flax exported. Immediately there was a storm of protest from Lancashire, which demonstrates better than any other evidence, how heavily the linen industry depended on supplies from Ireland. In reply the Queen granted a licence to a merchant named Edward Moore, allowing him to export three thousand packs of linen yarn, each weighing four hundred pounds.[4] This in its turn caused great dismay among the Irish linen workers, while on the other hand a petition supporting the grant was presented by the Lancashire workers. The petition was entitled 'the causes that maye move her Majestie to grante the lycense for transportinge of Irishe yarne into Englande'.[5] One of the reasons given was that

where upon the transportinge of the same yarne in tymes paste into the countries of Chester and Lancaster the poor people of the same cuntries especially aboute Manchester were set on worke to the reliefe of iiij^m persons within that lordship only . . . the same poor people for lacke of worke are utterlye impoverished living idely and redy to faule into miserable shiftes and extremityes.

Faced with opposition from both sides, the Queen attempted a compromise by reducing the grant to two thousand packs.[6] The needs of the Lancashire workers meant more to the government than those of the Irish, and as a result, similar grants continued to be made in spite of protests from the Irish. In 1591 for instance, permission was given to Richard Carmarden of London and his agents to take twelve hundred packs of yarn yearly to Bristol, Chester, or Liverpool. Each pack was to weigh four hundred pounds. The following year, eleven hundred and twenty-three packs were

[1] ibid., p. 78.   [2] ibid., p. 78.   [3] ibid., p. 78.
[4] R. H. Tawney and E. Power, *Tudor Economic Documents*, i, p. 189.
[5] ibid., i, p. 189.
[6] ibid., p. 189.

actually exported from Ireland.[1] In the last decade of the century there was an enormous increase over previous figures in the amounts of linen yarn leaving Ireland, as will soon be shown.

A large percentage of these Irish raw materials came into England through Liverpool. Leland noted that in 1535 'Irisch marchauntes cum much thither, as to a good haven. At Lyrpole is smaule custume payid that causithe marchantes to resorte. Good marchandis at Lyrpole, and moch Yrisch yarn that Manchester men do by ther.'[2] The Liverpool Port Books give some idea as to the quantities and values of these imports. Unfortunately, however, the Port Books do not include details of any of the illegal trade which inevitably took place when a particular branch of any trade was under restraint, but the figures given can at least be taken to represent the minimum amount of trade which went on.

The year beginning Michaelmas 1565 is the earliest date for which detailed statistics are available.[3] There was still at that date no restraint on linen yarn exports and during the year a total of three hundred and fifty-eight packs[4] of linen yarn were unloaded at Liverpool. The importance of Irish yarn imports to Liverpool's economy as a port is shown by the fact that out of fifty-two vessels which docked there in that year, forty-one carried packs of yarn, in varying quantities. Often the whole cargo consisted solely of yarn.

As for imports of wool from Ireland, the Port Books show that in the same year, beginning in Michaelmas 1565, one hundred and four stones of wool, and three hundred and thirty-three stones of flocks—the coarsest type of wool, were imported through Liverpool. It must be remembered that the prohibition on raw wool export from Ireland was still in force, which helps to explain the small amount. Some wool also came in the form of sheep fells—about five thousand arrived during the year.

The next year suitable for detailed study is that beginning Michaelmas 1572.[5] This is the time when the controversy resulting from the ban on linen yarn exports from Ireland was in full swing; it is, therefore, not surprising that there had been a very sharp fall in exports to a hundred and eighty-six packs. Three years later the problem had still not been resolved and the Lancashire linen workers must have found themselves in an even more unpleasant position; for in 1575/6 only one hundred and twelve and a half packs of linen yarn reached England through Liverpool.

[1] Longfield, op. cit., p. 91. This was the yarn exported under the grant, but other yarn was exported as well, see table on p. 24.

[2] Leland, op. cit., v, p. 41.

[3] 1565/6 is covered by two Port Books: E190, 1323/4; and E190, 1323/9.

[4] The units of this yarn are given in packs and fardels; it is obvious from the subsidies paid that a fardel contained half the amount of yarn in a full pack. Thus it was possible to arrive at a convenient figure in packs.

[5] E190, 1324/4.

The ban did not, of course, affect raw wool imports which continued to increase gradually.[1]

All is then blank for the next seven years until the year beginning Michaelmas 1582.[2] By that time, thanks to the licences granted by the Queen, the difficulties of the weavers had probably become less serious; linen yarn exports from Ireland recovered to the level of 1565—four hundred and twenty-three packs. On this occasion the clerk at the customs house actually took the trouble to mention that the commodity was linen yarn, not simply yarn. The Irish government's ban does not seem to have seriously interfered with the trade in linen yarn after this date.

Ten years later imports of yarn and wool had reached unprecedented heights. In the year beginning Michaelmas 1592[3] no fewer than one thousand four hundred and sixty-eight and a half packs of linen yarn passed through the customs house, together with one thousand eight hundred and seventy-eight stones of wool. The amount of flocks imported had fallen slightly to six hundred and fifty-four stones. By that time, out of a total of eighty vessels which entered the port, sixty carried Irish linen yarn, and again in many cases the whole cargo consisted of yarn. There can be no doubt that Liverpool's increasing prosperity and importance as a port was being fostered by the demands of the Manchester linen weavers. Imports of linen yarn continued to increase, and in the following year— 1593/4—they reached a new peak of one thousand five hundred and ten and a half packs.[4] However, in the early years of the sixteenth century, linen yarn imports did not maintain this high level. In 1602/3, for instance, they had fallen to four hundred and fifty-one and a half packs,[5] which although a somewhat drastic reduction, may be thought of as a more normal amount, in line with the years 1565/6 and 1582/3.[6]

Liverpool was not the only port to handle Irish goods. Chester also played a part and fortunately, Chester Port Books have survived for four of the years already examined in the case of Liverpool. In the first of these four years, 1565/6,[7] the amounts of raw materials imported through Chester were almost negligible.[8] By 1582/3[9] Chester's share in the trade had increased appreciably, and imports of linen yarn stood at ninety-three packs. Imports of raw wool consisted of two hundred and seven stones of wool and a hundred and six stones of flocks.

Ten years later[10] linen yarn imports had fallen to eighty-one packs, but

---

[1] The full figures are given in table 3.
[2] E190, 1325/1.
[3] E190, 1326/8.
[4] E190, 1326/26.
[5] E190, 1328/2.
[6] For an explanation of this fall in imports of linen yarn, see chapter 7, pp. 166–7.
[7] E190, 1323/1 and E190, 1323/10. On Chester's trade see D. M. Woodward, *The Trade of Elizabethan Chester* (1970).
[8] See table 3.
[9] E190, 1325/8.
[10] E190, 1328/5.

there had been a tremendous increase in the volume of raw wool, which was almost ten times greater and stood at over three thousand stones, much more than was handled at Liverpool in the same year. Even the imports of flocks had increased to more than seven times the 1582 figure. At the beginning of the seventeenth century Chester seems to have maintained her general level of linen yarn imports, unlike Liverpool. In 1602/3 the figure reached one hundred and seven and a half packs.[1]

Bald statements of quantities in different sorts of measures give no idea of the relative importance of the linen yarn and wool trade. Fortunately the Chester Port Books for 1582/3[2] and 1592/3,[3] as well as giving the subsidy paid on each import, also mention the value of some items. Unreliable though these values may be, they do enable some comparison to be made. A pack of linen yarn was invariably valued at £5 in 1582/3 and there had been no change by 1592. The same can be said for the price

Table 3. Imports of Irish raw materials.

		Liverpool	Chester
	linen yarn	358 packs	4 packs
1565/6	wool	104 stones	44 stones
	flocks	333 stones	80 stones
	linen yarn	186 packs	
1572/3	wool	116 stones	
	flocks	221 stones	
	linen yarn	112½ packs	
1575/6	wool	279 stones	
	flocks	366 stones	
	linen yarn	423 packs, value £2115	93 packs, value £465
1582/3	wool	450 stones⎫	207 stones⎫
		⎬value £127 7s.*	⎬value £40
	flocks	798 stones⎭	106 stones⎭
	linen yarn	1468½ packs, value £7342 10s.	81 packs, value £405
1592/3	wool	1878 stones⎫	3081 stones⎫
		⎬value £424 13s.	⎬value £681 3s.
	flocks	654 stones⎭	866 stones⎭
1593/4	linen yarn	1510½ packs, value £7552 10s.	
1602/3	linen yarn	451½ packs, value £2257 10s.	107½ packs, value £537 10s.

*The values of wool and flocks are maximum values arrived at by calculating each stone at the highest price given. It would have been impossible to work out the average price per stone; not every batch of wool has its value stated.

[1] E190, 1328/20.   [2] E190, 1325/8.   [3] E190, 1328/5.

of flocks, which was usually 1s. 6d. a stone and never more than that. The price of raw wool had increased slightly in the intervening ten years: in 1582 it ranged between 2s. 4d. and 3s. a stone, and in 1592 between 3s. and 4s. A few calculations give a very rough idea of the values of imports, which are given in table 3.

Inaccurate though these figures are, they do enable some broad conclusions to be made. The Lancashire linen weavers obviously relied fairly heavily on supplies of Irish linen yarn and were far more dependent on Ireland than the woollen manufacturers were. As the century progressed it was Liverpool which became increasingly more important in handling the linen yarn trade, although Chester did maintain her much lower level of imports during the first decade of the seventeenth century, whereas at the same time, the boom in the Liverpool import trade had ended.

In addition to this, the figures seem to suggest that during the last fifteen years or so of the century the linen industry underwent some considerable and rapid expansion, judging by the vast increase in the volume of yarn needed to feed it.

As far as the woollen industry is concerned, the last ten years of the century saw its workers possibly more dependent on Irish wool than before. At least the Chester figures suggest this. One also finds, for instance, that George Holt, a Salford clothier who in 1598 had a large stock of about a hundred and fifty stones of wool, had obtained almost one third of this stock from Ireland.[1] On the other hand, in 1592/3, imports of raw wool through Liverpool were no more than 5% of all the raw materials handled by that port during the year. It is probably true to say that although the trend had begun, Ireland as a source of wool did not become of crucial importance to the Lancashire industry until well on in the seventeenth century.[2]

The bulk of the importing of raw materials from Ireland was carried out by Irish merchants. During that first year for which Liverpool Port Books exist,[3] beginning at Michaelmas 1565, well over fifty Irish merchants took part in the trade, dealing mostly in linen yarn, for the wool trade was still a very minor branch of their activities. Most of these men appear at least twice during the year, and several of them, such as Simon Grove of Dublin, Nicholas Gough of Aboy and Robert Carus of Drogheda, appear five or six times each. The usual practice was for a merchant to divide his goods among a number of ships as a precaution against shipwreck, which would hit him hard if one ship carrying all his goods happened to be lost in a storm. Thus on May 29th, 1566, the tiny 'Saviour',

[1] infra, ch. iii, p. 32.
[2] The wool import figures cannot include wool in the form of sheep fells. However, it seems doubtful whether the amounts of wool concerned would affect the general conclusion. This is borne out by Bowden who points out (p. 71) that Ireland did not become an important wool source for Lancashire until mid-seventeenth century.
[3] E190, 1323/4 and E190, 1323/9.

a Liverpool vessel of only twenty-four tons, arrived from Dublin with a cargo of five packs of linen yarn and five hundred sheep fells, belonging to four Irish merchants.

It was not entirely unknown, however, for a Lancashire man to travel to Ireland and buy raw materials there. In 1528 William Walker, a Liverpool merchant, was in Ireland attempting to smuggle wool out of the country in order to evade the recent prohibition. He bought 'two greate packes of wool to the value of twenty poundes', and brought them to Liverpool.[1] Unfortunately for him his activities did not pass undetected and a writ of the Duchy Court ordered him to surrender the wool or pay a fine of £10.

Nor was the legitimate trade monopolised by the Irish. Richard Fox was a Manchester merchant who regularly imported Irish raw materials. The Port Books[2] show that on eight separate occasions in the year beginning Michaelmas 1565 he imported linen yarn through Liverpool. He dealt with a total of seventeen and three quarter packs and also with twenty stones of wool and thirty stones of flocks. Moreover, at the same time, a Chester merchant, Robert Brerewood, was acting as an agent for Fox at Chester, where he imported one pack of linen yarn in Fox's name.[3] For close on thirty years Fox continued to be a regular importer of linen yarn and wool, and usually had other men acting as his agents at Chester. On April 11th, 1583, for instance, John Fox brought in two and a half packs of yarn under Richard's name.[4] The last surviving mention of Richard Fox is in the Liverpool Port Book for 1592/3.[5]

No other Lancashire merchant equalled the record of Richard Fox. Several others imported raw materials but do not seem to have made a regular habit of it. Very rarely does a name appear more than once in the Port Books. However, it will be worthwhile to mention a few of these men. The only other Lancashire merchant whose name appears more than once in any one year was Richard Harrison of Manchester; his transactions were modest in comparison with those of Fox; he confined himself to wool. On three occasions in 1565/6[6] he imported small amounts of flocks making a total of forty-six stones; but his name does not appear again. Another Manchester man, Francis Pendleton, was responsible for importing forty stones of flocks and wool in the same year. Entered under the date September 27th, 1576,[7] is the name Edward Baxter, also of Manchester, who brought a quarter of a pack of linen yarn into Liverpool.

The year 1592/3[8] saw quite a number of Lancashire merchants trading in a modest way at Liverpool. There was first of all Simon Malon of

---

[1] D.L.3/5. M2.
[2] E190, 1323/4 and E190, 1323/9.   [3] E190, 1323/1.
[4] E190, 1325/8.   [5] E190, 1326/8.
[6] E190, 1323/4 and E190, 1323/9.   [7] E190, 1324/9.
[8] E190, 1326/8.

Manchester who imported fifty stones of wool all in one large batch on May 3rd, 1593. At the same time Malon had some sort of agreement with a Dublin merchant named John Varden, who imported sixty stones of wool and flocks and three hundred sheep fells on Malon's behalf at Chester. Richard Ashton was a merchant who had travelled slightly further than the others—from Ashton-under-Lyne. Yet all he imported was a mere eighteen stones of flocks. Finally two Liverpool merchants are mentioned: John Shelton imported ninety-two stones of wool and flocks, and Thomas Fletcher a pack of linen yarn.

It is noticeable that there was a group of men who came to deal in the wool trade perhaps almost accidentally. These were the glovers and leathersellers who used to buy large quantities of sheep skins among other types of skins as a normal part of their business. The wool on the skin was of no use in the leather industry, so it was sold to wool dealers and to manufacturers.[1] It was only a short step from selling superfluous wool to dealing in fleece wool, and more than one leather merchant took the step in the second half of the sixteenth century. Simon Malon is a good example of this group; he has already been seen importing skins through Chester and wool through Chester and Liverpool. He used the skins for making gloves, some of which were exported back to Ireland. Thus on February 5th, 1601, one finds Malon sending six dozen pairs of 'Manchester gloves' valued at £6, through Liverpool to Dublin.[2]

Another example is Robert Brerewood of Chester who handled small quantities of wool alongside his main occupation of importing fells. On March 26th, 1566, he imported ten stones of wool, but the main items were thirteen hundred sheep fells and a thousand 'broke' fells.[3] Two Wigan merchants appear to have been engaged in a similar business, their main concern being with fells, with a sideline in small quantities of fleece wool. James Banks is mentioned twice in 1592, and brought into Liverpool nine stones of wool and twelve hundred sheep fells. Ralph Barrow was the other Wigan man trading at Liverpool in the same year, and concerned with very small quantities: twelve stones of flocks and three hundred sheep fells.[4]

There are one or two other Lancashire merchants in the Port Books, and even, on two occasions, Kendal merchants.[5] But it must be emphasised that these are comparatively rare; the bulk of the trade was handled by the Irish.

Once the Irish raw materials had arrived in England, there were several ways in which they might continue their journey to the industrial areas of Lancashire. Those Lancashire merchants such as Fox, Baxter,

---

[1] Bowden, p. 82. [2] E190, 1327/30.
[3] E190, 1323/1 and E190, 1323/10.
[4] E190, 1326/8.
[5] In 1565 (E190, 1323/4) and 1573 (E190, 1324/4).

Malon, and Pendleton who imported wool or yarn, would presumably transport it to Manchester themselves, where it would be sold in the merchant's shop or at the local fair. Francis Pendleton had his own shop in Manchester where he sold wool and linen yarn.[1]

Perhaps the most common procedure was for the Irish merchant himself to travel inland and bring the yarn to Manchester. This is suggested by the preamble to the Act of 1542[2] which removed the sanctuary from Manchester to Chester and which mentions that 'many straungers as well of Irlond as of other places within this Realme have reasorted to the said towne (Manchester) with lynnen yarne woolles and other necessary wares for making of clothes'. Thomas Money, a Dublin merchant, was one of these 'straungers' who made a regular habit of transporting Irish yarn which he 'usuallye uttered and solde aboute the towne of Manchestre'.[3] He was there in 1591 when he had with him large quantities of linen yarn, some of which he sold to Giles Hilton of Oldham, a prosperous weaver.[4] The price was £26 to be paid at a later date. According to Hilton the money was duly paid. Knowledge of the transaction has survived only because a dispute arose when the Irishman claimed that Hilton had failed to pay, whereupon the latter brought a suit against Money in the Court of Requests. This case, as well as providing an illustration of an Irish merchant trading in Manchester, also demonstrates how local dealers and prosperous weavers who lived in the small towns outside Manchester itself, must have come into Manchester to buy yarn, the town thus serving as a general centre for raw materials. Moreover, men from even further afield came to Manchester for the same purpose. A representative of the Shuttleworth family of Gawthorpe Hall near Burnley, was in Manchester in 1589, when he bought a quarter of a pack of Irish linen yarn.[5]

On the other hand, some Manchester merchants and dealers, though not ambitious enough to import raw materials themselves, were not content to sit at home and allow the Irishmen to monopolise the trade. Leland thought it a common procedure for Manchester men to be in Liverpool buying Irish yarn.[6] There is also an interesting case in the Duchy Court of Lancaster in 1530,[7] which gives a momentary glimpse of the sort of activity which went on. Three Manchester men, John Travis, Perres Bowker and Geoffrey Bowker, made a contract with Thomas Beck to carry and deliver to them 'the number of so myche Irysh woll as shuld cum to the seyd sum', of twenty pounds, at 2s. 2d. a stone. They paid Beck the £20 before he left Manchester. One is given the impression that the men were expecting a specific batch of wool to arrive in Liverpool

[1] Will and inventory of Francis Pendleton, 1574.
[2] 33 Henry VIII, cap. 15.   [3] Req. 2/110/32.
[4] *infra*, ch. iv, pp. 48–9.   [5] *Shuttleworth Accounts*, i, p. 55.
[6] Leland, op. cit., v, p. 41.
[7] *Pleadings and Depositions, Duchy Court of Lancaster*, i, p. 227; ed. H. Fishwick.

and that some agreement about purchase had already been made with the importing merchant, for the contract goes on to mention that if the wool were taken or lost by sea Beck should return the money. Perhaps they were expecting smuggled wool which was in danger of being seized by the customs officers. They were not entirely happy about the character of Beck. 'The said Thomas was poore and of no greate substance', so a man called Nicholas Blake agreed to stand surety for him. He must have regretted this later when Beck failed both to deliver the wool and to repay the £20.

It was in ways such as these, at least when transactions worked out as planned, that the first stage in the long process of cloth manufacture was achieved: supplies of raw materials had been obtained, by a variety of possible methods. Prosperous linen weavers like Giles Hilton could buy yarn from Irish merchants in Manchester; other weavers could buy from local merchants who had themselves bought the yarn in Liverpool, or who had had supplies brought up from the south. Woollen weavers of the more successful type probably used similar methods. In their case there was also the possibility that they had grown their own wool or had bought it from a local grower. As for the poorer weavers who only needed small quantities of raw materials at a time, they would be able to buy what they needed at the local fair and from travelling broggers. But this is tending to stray onto another topic—the question of the relationship between weavers and the men who supplied them with raw materials. This will be discussed later.

CHAPTER III

THE ORGANISATION OF THE
WOOLLEN INDUSTRY

THE organisation of the textile industry can best be described by dealing firstly with the woollen manufacture, and secondly with linen. This survey of both the woollen and linen industries is based on the inventories of every Lancashire man in the sixteenth century who called himself clothier, weaver, shearman, fuller, dyer or clothworker. Unfortunately this is not so impressive as it sounds, because the industrial activities of many Lancashire men were disguised under the name of yeoman or husbandman. There are only sixty-five wills surviving with inventories of men whose stated occupation was one connected with cloth manufacture and trade and who died in the sixteenth century. In addition, a further sixty-five have been discovered who were actively engaged in the textile industry but whose occupation is either not stated at all, or given as yeoman or husbandman.

From these wills and inventories and from several other important documents concerned with woollen manufacture in Lancashire, a fairly clear picture emerges of how the industry was organised. It is clear that certainly in the first eighty years of the century the majority of woollen manufacturers were quite poor men who worked at home, assisted by the rest of the family, and who owned one loom and perhaps a spinning wheel. They were usually small scale farmers as well, and though poor, were completely independent. They bought wool in small quantities of a stone or so at a time, probably on credit, from wool dealers or broggers, as they were called. They were free to sell their product to the best buyer, being under no obligation to return the cloth to the dealer who had supplied them with raw materials. The Act of 1542[1] which removed the sanctuary from Manchester to Chester because it was undesirable to have large numbers of criminals wandering about Manchester now that the textile industry was developing, seems to be quite clear on this point. The

[1] 33 Henry VIII, cap. 15.

preamble to the Act shows that basically the organisation of both woollen and linen industries was the same:

Many straungers as well of Irlond as of other places within this Realme have reasorted to the said towne with lynnen yarne woolles and other necessary wares for making of clothes to be sold there, and have used to credite and truste the pore inhabitaunts of the same towne, whiche were not able and had not redy money to pay in hand for the said yarnes wolles and wares, unto suche tyme the said credites with theire industry labour and paynes myght make clothes of the said wolles yarne and other necessary wares, and sold the same to content and pay their Creditours.

It is plain from this that they came into contact with two different middlemen; the dealer who bought the cloth was not the man who supplied them with the raw materials. This state of affairs could be expected to continue for so long as the small manufacturers had unhindered access to the middlemen wool dealers. Details have survived of many transactions in which weavers bought wool from dealers on credit. James Roberts of Ightenhill, near Burnley, bought wool and lambs worth 46s. from the Abbot of Whalley in 1508.[1] In 1523 a weaver named Christopher Parkinson bought wool worth £4 15s. from a dealer called Lister at Rimington.[2] Five years later, a case at Tottington Halmote reveals Charles Ramsbottom selling wool for 22s. to Edward Lomax, who had failed to pay for it.[3] Often the amounts of wool involved were very small indeed: in Accrington two men bought quantities worth 6s. 8d. and 6s.[4] It was not only the dealer who suffered, for there were dishonest dealers as well as customers. One dealer appeared in court at Tottington Halmote in 1515 and was fined 6d. for keeping a light weight for weighing wool.[5]

In the middle of the century the position of the poorer weavers became less secure. The supply line which the wool dealers provided was suddenly threatened by government interference. In 1551 and 1552 the sudden slump in cloth exports from England seriously affected merchant interests, especially those of the Merchant Adventurers and the Staplers, who demanded interference by the government to restrict the growth of the industry and the increase in the numbers of middlemen who were permitting the industry to expand. The resulting contraction of the industry would, they hoped, reduce the demand for wool and therefore the price of wool. Middlemen had been much criticised because they were suspected of causing the rise in wool prices by buying up and withholding available supplies; thus an attack on their activities would be another way of reducing wool prices, and would cut off many small producers from their raw material supply, thus forcing them out of business and preventing further expansion of the industry.

[1] *C.C.R.*, ii, p. 22.   [2] ibid., p. 278.   [3] *C.C.R.*, iii, p. 303.
[4] ibid., iii, p. 33; p. 130.   [5] ibid., iii, p. 282.

In Lancashire there was a certain amount of trouble from forestallers, some of whom appeared in court. In 1522 six people were fined one shilling each at Tottington Halmote. It was stated that they 'gravely hindered the market at Bury, and bought wool and other merchandise before coming thither'. They were found guilty of being 'common regrators and forestallers'.[1] The following year seven people were fined at Tottington for exactly similar offences, but this time the fine was 1s. 4d.[2] There were no more cases of this nature at Tottington Halmote until 1541 when three men were fined 2s. each for forestalling wool.[3] Three people were fined 1s. each at Accrington Halmote in 1540; they had been breaking the law for a year and were found guilty of being 'common forestallers of the King's markets in Lancashire'.[4]

Accordingly in 1552 the government passed an Act to bring down the price of wool.[5] It was expressly directed against middlemen and forbade the buying of wool from the grower except by authentic Staplers or by cloth manufacturers. This was not the first time that middleman activities had been attacked by the government,[6] but the 1552 measures were much the most stringent. If this act had been enforced, the small Lancashire manufacturers, along with their counterparts in other areas of England, would have been cut off from distant wool supplies and would have become dependent on a few wealthy manufacturers who could afford to bring large quantities of wool from a distance, a situation which had already developed in Wiltshire.[7]

In the sixteenth century, however, it was one thing to pass a statute, but quite another to make sure that it was enforced. The further away a district was from London, the more difficult did the Tudor government find it to make its wishes felt in that district, no matter what aspect of legislation was involved. The effective enforcement of such restrictive legislation as the 1552 Act was bound to be difficult, if not impossible. The government soon came to realise that local conditions, especially in the North of England, where the wool middleman was an essential link, required special consideration. For this reason, in 1555 wool broggers were allowed to operate in the parish of Halifax.[8] Bills to permit similar activities in Lancashire and the rest of Yorkshire were rejected in 1562 and 1563.[9] But the situation probably did not become too serious until 1576. Up to that date, thanks to a reasonably good state of trade, the Act was enforced laxly. The Crown granted a series of licences permitting it

---

[1] *C.C.R.*, p. 290.   [2] ibid., p. 292.   [3] ibid., p. 331.

[4] ibid., p. 112.   [5] 5 and 6 Edward VI, cap. 7.

[6] Similar acts had been passed in 1531 (22 Henry VIII, cap. 1.) and in 1546 (37 Henry VIII, cap. 15).

[7] G. D. Ramsay, *The Wiltshire Woollen Industry in the Sixteenth and Seventeenth Centuries*, p. 14 passim.

[8] 2 and 3 Philip and Mary, cap. 13.

[9] *House of Commons Journals*, i, pp. 2, 4, 29, 34, 43, 44, 48, 70, 71–2, 73, 74, 77, 78, 79.

to be infringed,[1] and in 1576 it was reported to Elizabeth's secretary that the statute had fallen into disuse.[2] There is no reason to doubt that wool broggers were as active in Lancashire as elsewhere.

In 1576, however, the government decided to act again. The price of wool was still increasing and there was agitation against wool middlemen; so in November, 1576, all licences for the sale of wool were cancelled, and the following February it was demanded that all J.P.s should co-operate in enforcing the measure.[3]

Faced with this stiffer attitude on the part of the government, the clothiers of Lancashire and of several other northern counties sent a petition to the Privy Council in October 1577. This document[4] shows that at this date the majority of Lancashire clothiers were still quite poor but had maintained their independence. They describe themselves as cottagers whose 'habylitie wyll not stretche neyther to buye any substance of wolles to maynteyne worke and labor, nor yet to fetche the same, the growyth (of) wolles beyng foure and fyve skore myles att the least'. They were afraid of two results if the legislation were enforced. Firstly there was the danger that the people of Halifax who were permitted wool middlemen by the Act of 1555, would use this liberty to 'wynne the trade of euerye cuntrye into their owne handes'. Secondly they feared that without direct access to the wool dealer, the trade would be driven 'into a fewe ryche men's handes. . . . The pore shall not be paide for theire worke, but as it pleaseth the ryche, and the clothe shall reste in their hands to sell at their pleasure.'

This request was not granted,[5] and for some time the small cottagers must have felt the pinch. But this was probably only temporary, for within a few months the government allowed licensed dealers to operate again. Until 1588 the Privy Council's attitude to middlemen became more tolerant; trade was reasonably good, there had been no further increase in the price of wool, and dealers continued to buy and sell wool very much as they had previously.[6] There is no doubt at all that in Lancashire wool broggers continued to be active until the end of the sixteenth century.

The best example of a wool dealer is that of Robert Birkenshaw of Gorton, near Manchester, who was active until his death in 1587. He sold wool in widely varying quantities. On the one hand he had sold a whole pack of wool worth £8 18s. on credit to George Gledell; on the other hand a man named Richard Rogerson had bought wool from him worth £2 10s., also on credit. Birkenshaw was concerned purely with selling the raw materials, and did not buy cloth from weavers. He did not confine himself to selling raw wool, however, but dealt in flax, and had sold horses, malt, oxen, beans, and just before his death, a hat with a

[1] Bowden, p. 130. [2] Ramsay, op. cit., p. 10. [3] Bowden, p. 135.
[4] P.R.O. S.P. 12/117/38. Quoted by Wadsworth and Mann, p. 7.
[5] Bowden, p. 142. [6] ibid., p. 141.

C

feather in it.[1] A dealer who supplied wool in small quantities was Lawrence Parker of Colne, who died in 1597. Like Birkenshaw he sold other commodities as well as wool, and his stock included small amounts of cloth, thread, combs, buttons, and gloves. When he died he had just over four stones of wool in stock, worth £1 3s. 4d.

In 1588 some wool broggers operating at Rochdale were prosecuted; there was an immediate outcry from the small producers who put forward all the old arguments, showing that the majority of them were still poor but independent. If middlemen were prohibited, they said, 'ther were thousandes of poore people utterlie undone'.[2] The Privy Council was sympathetic and decided in their favour, announcing that 'Northern men shall have libertie to sell woolle in the towne of Ratchdall to any person .... which will buye the same. . . . But let the same buyer be well advised he sell not the same again, but converte it into clothe.'[3]

In the rest of Lancashire, we know that broggers were active, even though no specific exception was made by the government. In July 1590 the Crown granted a patent to Simon Bowyer,[4] which allowed him the right to be sole informer against all unauthorised wool dealers. However, the government apparently looked on this grant not as a means of preventing middlemen from trading, but primarily as a fiscal expedient to raise money. Dealers were to pay a fine, of which half went to the Crown and half to Bowyer. But he had too few agents, and so many dealers were missed. Some Lancashire wool dealers were among those who were slow to pay Mr. Bowyer the required amount. As a result, the Privy Council wrote to some officials in Lancashire, asking them to instruct all wool dealers who had not already compounded with the patentee, to do so at once.[5] Provided the dealers could afford the payments which Bowyer demanded, they would be able to continue their business.

At the end of the century, in 1602 to be exact, after the termination of Bowyer's patent, Sir John Hoby was granted a similar patent which gave him the right to sell licences to wool dealers in many counties of England.[6] There was a great deal of opposition to this patent from wealthy capitalist clothiers who feared it might enable poor weavers to escape from their domination. The government, however, seemed to have realised the necessity for middlemen in some areas, and so Hoby was only allowed to grant licences in counties where the cloth industry was not organised on capitalistic lines, thus not offending capitalist clothiers, while at the same time allowing small weavers to continue trading with middlemen. It is

[1] Will and inventory of Robert Birkenshaw, 1587. In this chapter, and throughout the remainder of the book, all information about people in the textile industry, unless its source is otherwise stated, was obtained from the will or inventory of the person concerned. All these documents are in the Lancashire County Record Office at Preston.

[2] *Historical MSS. Commission, Kenyon MSS.*, p. 595.

[3] ibid., p. 595.   [4] Bowden, p. 147.   [5] ibid., p. 148.

[6] ibid., p. 149.

significant that Lancashire was one of the counties in which Hoby was allowed to collect money from wool broggers for licences.[1] Many managed to continue trading without a licence; one of the agents complained to Hoby that wool dealers 'concealed themselves' from him.[2]

The fears of the small Lancashire woollen clothiers were therefore probably not fully realised. There could well be some exaggeration in their complaints, a deliberate overstating of the case in order to impress the authorities. It was simply not true for instance, as we have already seen, to claim that the nearest growth of wool was eighty miles away. It must not be forgotten that many Lancashire clothiers themselves kept sheep. Two Colne men with a hundred and sixty sheep between them have already been mentioned.[3] Robert Ravald of Kearsley, a producer of Manchester cottons, kept about thirty sheep. William Fletcher of Bury, who died in 1602 and spent much time carding and spinning wool, owned well over a hundred sheep valued at £13. Men who kept sheep in such numbers would be able to supply themselves with far from negligible amounts of wool. One hundred sheep could provide between fourteen and twenty stones of wool, depending on the weight of the fleece,[4] and twenty stones of wool was enough to make ten kerseys, which would keep a weaver occupied for two months.[5] One would expect to find that most of the small clothiers, in spite of temporary spells of difficulty and anxiety, managed to maintain their independence. If many of them did find themselves in an uncomfortable position shortly after 1585, this was caused not so much by lack of wool dealers as by lack of markets for their products—hostilities on the continent of Europe, and to some extent the war with Spain, seriously hampered overseas trade.[6]

It is possible to quote examples of every class and occupation in the woollen industry. The first processes carried out in woollen cloth manufacture were greasing and carding. The raw wool was thoroughly oiled or greased with butter, and then carded, by being placed in handfuls between a pair of hand cards, or between one hand card and a fixed stock card, and worked about in all directions until the fibres were interlocked into a close, fluffy mass, ready for spinning. First of all then, there was a large group of people, possibly the largest single group in the whole of the woollen industry, who specialised in carding and spinning. It is known that it took at least five people working full time at greasing, carding and spinning, to keep one weaver fully supplied with yarn,[7] and although many clothiers kept one or two spinning wheels and some pairs of wool cards, not all of them would have been able to produce enough yarn to

[1] ibid., p. 150.   [2] ibid., p. 150.   [3] supra, ch. ii, p. 1.
[4] supra, ch. ii, p. 10.
[5] H. Heaton, The Yorkshire Woollen and Worsted Industry, p. 108.
[6] infra, ch. v, pp. 66–8.
[7] Historical MSS. Commission, Kenyon MSS., p. 573. Quoted in Heaton, op. cit., p. 108.

keep the loom fully supplied, even if the whole family was involved. Carding was apparently an unpleasant and arduous job which would not normally be done by women or children. Thus a weaver would resort to the army of workers who did no more than transform wool into yarn. Most women spent part of their time spinning; it was the traditional occupation, and it is very rare to come across the inventory of a woman who did not keep a spinning wheel.

One of the men who bought wool, carded and spun it, and then presumably sold it to a weaver, was John Clegg of Newbold hamlet, Rochdale. When he died in 1587 he had at least two spinning wheels, and wool cards and combs. He also had some raw wool, and wool already spun into yarn, the total value of which was £15, almost half his total wealth of £31. He did not own a loom, and had no cloth in his house. Three cows valued at £5 helped his family economy. Two men owed him sums of money, one £2 8s., the other 10s., which may well have been for yarn which they had bought from him.

William Greenhalgh of Prestwich, Manchester, who died in 1597, was another member of this class of clothworkers, living in similar circumstances. He was worth about £30, and kept two spinning wheels, cards, combs, and combstocks, but no loom. There was black and white wool and yarn in the house, worth £4 6s. 8d. His agricultural activities were more extensive than Clegg's. Livestock—cows and horses—were worth over £10, and he had just sold a bushel of meal to John Bradshaw, Esquire.

Sometimes the owner of a few sheep converted his own wool into yarn before selling it to a weaver. Henry Mitton was a prosperous Colne yeoman who kept twenty-three sheep. He owned two spinning wheels and wool cards and at the time of his death in 1597 there was raw wool and yarn in the house worth £1. In 1605 John Lomax of Bury owned well over seventy sheep and kept spinning wheels, cards and combs, but no looms.

On occasion, though this seems to have been confined to the Colne area, a man would card and spin the wool into yarn and then set up the yarn into a warp which he sold to a weaver, thus saving that weaver a great deal of time and trouble. Lawrence Mitton, of Great Marsden, near Colne, who died in 1558, spent much of his time carding and spinning wool, and was probably an active wool brogger, having forty-four stones in stock valued at £15 13s. 8d. He also had two warps worth 13s. 4d. but did no weaving himself. Another example of this activity is provided by John Pollard, a Foulridge yeoman. At his death in 1608 he owned wool and yarn worth almost £5, and had just sold a warp for 9s. to a weaver named John Hartley.

The weavers themselves were a varied class of workers. The majority of them were poor but independent, some were slightly more prosperous than others; some were even higher on the scale of wealth, and at the top of the pyramid there was a small group of weavers who had developed their activities to such an extent that by the end of the century they had become employers of labour on a small scale. Since the majority of weavers were poor, probably only a small percentage of them could afford to have a will written, and it is more difficult to quote specific examples of poorer weavers than it is to find the more prosperous ones. Enough wills have survived, however, to bear out what could already be surmised from the other evidence.

Richard Walwork was a Manchester weaver who must have been typical of hundreds of others in the same area. When he died in 1592 his possessions were worth about £30. He had a loom, warpstocks and wool valued at almost £2, but no cards or spinning wheels. He may well have sold the cloth made immediately before he fell ill, since the inventory makes no mention of any in the house. As well as weaving, Walwork must have spent much of his time in agriculture. He had a plough, harrows, carts, five cows and three horses, and had grown wheat, oats, and barley valued at £10. Not surprisingly, he still looked on himself as a farmer rather than as a weaver, and had himself described as a 'husbandman' in his will.

This division of activity between cloth production and agriculture was extremely common in Lancashire, and with few exceptions, every weaver, rich and poor alike, spent some of his time in the fields. If the state of the market for his woollen cloth was good, he would probably concentrate on weaving and take full advantage of the opportunity for extra profit. On the other hand, one of the frequent short slumps in the cloth trade might not mean complete disaster for him; he could manage to exist on his farming until the markets improved.

Edward Butterworth was a husbandman who lived at Rochdale and died in 1598. His total wealth, when a few debts had been settled, amounted to a little short of £17. He carried out all the initial processes of cloth manufacture, as well as weaving, and owned a loom, at least two spinning wheels, wool cards and combs, and had cloth and wool in the house, valued at £4 10s. The whole family would be kept busy spinning and carding the wool, while Butterworth himself worked at the loom. As for agriculture, there were cows and crops worth £11. His cottage was only sparsely furnished; apart from the loom and spinning wheels, there were only chests, a board serving as a table, a couple of stools and the beds, although he did have bedding valued at £3 6s. 8d., an unexpected luxury for a poor husbandman. His own clothes were worth 13s. 4d.

Two other Rochdale men had managed to make more money than Butterworth, and stood in the next rank, of slightly richer clothiers. The first of these was James Deurden, a prosperous smallholder of Stoneheys, a hamlet in the hills. The total value of all his goods was £59 4s., which included wool worth £20, and one loom with wool cards and combs. The second man was Nicholas Chadwick of Newbold hamlet, whose circumstances were very similar to Deurden's in almost every respect. The total value of goods listed in the inventory taken in 1593 was about £60, of which £26 was in fifty-two stones of wool and yarn; again, all stages of manufacture up to the actual weaving were carried out. Chadwick owned spinning wheels, cards, combs, combstocks, and a loom. His inventory also mentions a cart, ploughs, harrows, axes and 'other husbandry gear', various cattle and a pig, worth over £10 altogether, and crops worth £3 10s. Although he obviously spent some time in agriculture, Chadwick probably spent more time manufacturing cloth; it is significant that his industrial capital made up almost half his total wealth.

Another important centre of woollen cloth production was Blackburn. John Broxopp lived there and when he died in 1582, his inventory described him as a 'cotton man'. He was one of the rare people who relied entirely on weaving for a living, and did not keep even a cow. Yet he seems to have managed well enough. His possessions were valued at about £18. He had the usual loom 'to weave woollen clothe in', and thirty-five stones of wool and woollen yarn worth £14. There was no cloth actually in the house, but there was a large debt of £22 10s. 8d. owing to him, which could well have been for cloth sold by him on credit, and which helps to make his financial position rather more healthy.

A final example of a small-scale cloth producer is provided by John Pollard of Habergham Eaves, in the parish of Burnley, who died in 1592. He called himself a clothier, although he seems to have been more of a farmer than a clothier. Of his total wealth of about £50, £31 was in agricultural stock. But he did manufacture some cloth and carried out almost all the processes under his own roof, going so far as to shear and finish his cloth. He owned spinning wheels, cards, combs, three pairs of shears, two looms, and finally a stock of wool and yarn worth £2 8s. His two looms do not seem to have made him any more prosperous than the weavers who had only one. The fact is that a loom in itself was not expensive to build, and often they were valued at only a few shillings. Nicholas Chadwick's loom was only worth 2s. 6d. even with all its accessories. What determined a clothier's wealth was not so much how many looms he owned, but rather how intensively he used his looms. It may be true that some weavers liked to keep a spare loom about in reserve.

All these men are examples of what may be termed the lower ranks of weavers, whose wealth might be anything up to fifty or sixty pounds. Above these men there was another group, far fewer in number, who might almost be described as middle-class weavers. There is, however, no rigid division between the classes; they merge into each other, and some weavers seem to hover between the two. The typical middle-class weaver was one who had slightly more capital behind him, and could afford to buy a stock of raw materials big enough to occupy him for the next three or four months. He could probably afford also to employ one or two apprentices outside his own family. The wealth of such men often amounted to over £100.

The best example of this class of weaver was John Nabbs of Manchester, who died in 1570 and called himself a clothmaker. The total value of his goods was about £105, of which well over half was in industrial capital. He had a hundred and eighty stones of wool in the house, worth £36, and nineteen pieces of cloth valued at £25. His equipment consisted of three pairs of stock cards, three pairs of hand cards, spinning wheels, a loom, a shearboard, and shears. Thus every process except those of fulling and dyeing was carried on in the house. As far as one can make out from the will, he was either a bachelor or a widower, and had no children; so he employed six people whom he called servants, who must have worked full time, carding and spinning the wool and later shearing the cloth after Nabbs himself had woven it. This is probably the clue to his prosperity. The whole household was entirely geared to cloth manufacture; there was no time off to plough a field or to reap the corn, although he did own two cows and some hay. Thus even though he had only one loom he could make a comfortable living. His prosperity is reflected in the amount of money he was able to lay out in extra luxuries above the ordinary necessities. His own clothes were considered to be worth £2 and he could afford bedding worth £4. He even had £2 in ready money in the house, and in his will he left each of his six servants 5s. and requested that 'William and Nicholas the walkmens shall have 12d. each'.

Robert Ravald of Kearsley, near Manchester, was another clothworker who can be thought of as belonging to the middle class. He died in 1578 and had been occupied in producing Manchester cottons, although he still looked on himself as a yeoman farmer. Even so, his industrial capital and the debts owing to him for cloth made up well over one third of his total wealth of just under £90. He owned a loom, wool and woollen yarn worth 13s., and one piece of cottons priced at £1 3s. 4d. The most important item was a debt of £31 16s. owing to him from two men who had recently bought from him thirty pieces of cottons. The date fixed for payment of the debt was 'the feast Daye of Philippe and Jacob next'. He was fortunate in owning some sheep—possibly thirty[1]—which would provide him with some of his raw materials. He could expect somewhere between four and six stones of short wool each time his flock was sheared. Other animals were a yoke of oxen, four cows and two horses, all of which, together with the sheep, were valued at £25 10s. He had grown oats and barley worth just over £7. Thus his wealth was distributed almost equally between woollen cloth manufacture and agriculture, and unlike John

[1] See Appendix, p. 101.

Nabbs, he did not bother with the early processes of cloth production. He kept no spinning wheel, wool cards or shears, and does not seem to have employed other workers outside his own family.

These middle-class clothiers were not confined to the Manchester area. In Great Harwood for instance, lived Thomas Lache, who called himself a woollen weaver, and who carried out all processes of cloth manufacture except fulling, dyeing and shearing. The inventory of his goods taken after his death in 1590 shows that he owned cards, combs, spinning wheels and a loom, together with cloth, wool and yarn valued at £15. As usual, though he might call himself a weaver, he was busy with agriculture and kept a plough, a cart, a harrow, spades, a scythe, cattle and a pig, which, along with the crops he had grown were worth a total of almost £18. Altogether Lache would have been worth £80, when a number of debts, which may well have been for cloth, had been paid to him.

A clothier who worked on a slightly larger scale was Alban Lache, also of Great Harwood, who died in 1594. The total value of all his goods and money was over £110, and all processes except fulling and dyeing were done at the house. In addition to all the usual equipment—cards, combs, spinning wheels, shears and cloth presses—Lache kept a set of tenters for stretching the cloth back to its original size after it had been fulled. Unlike the clothiers mentioned so far, he kept three looms, and although there were only small amounts of wool and woollen cloth worth £2 in the house when he died, he had just sold cloth worth £44 to a dealer named Henry Robinson. For once the inventory leaves no doubt that the debt was for cloth. Thus again, in Lache's case, well over one third of his total wealth lay in his industrial capital and in debts for cloth sold. But he obviously did not spend all his time producing cloth; all three looms were certainly not kept busy continually, otherwise a much greater proportion of his wealth would have been in cloth. He was a substantial farmer, holding land on lease worth £8 12s. a year, and owning cattle worth £18, and pigs, horses, wheat, barley and hay. His agricultural capital was worth £35 altogether.

Another Lancashire clothier of the middle class who deserves mention was Richard Hamore of Whittaker, who died in 1594. His wealth was similar to that of Alban Lache, the total amounting to just over £107. He had wool and cloth valued at almost £25. Hamore managed to earn his living by using only one loom, and does not appear to have done any carding or spinning, or dressing of cloth. He depended less on agriculture which made up only £14 of his total wealth. It may well be that Hamore had recently received payment for some cloth sold, since he had the large sum of £25 in cash.

One final example who manages to scrape into the ranks of the middle class was John Driver of Bradley, in the parish of Colne. He looked on himself primarily as a clothier and must have spent most of his time manufacturing kersey cloth on his loom. When he died in 1597 there were over £18 worth of kerseys, and wool and yarn valued at over £7 in the house. He was awaiting payment of a debt of £11 13s. 8d. for cloth sold to Henry Robinson, the same man who bought cloth from Alban Lache at Great Harwood. This means that about half of Driver's total wealth of £72 was made up of cloth and raw materials.

All these middle-class clothiers, but more especially John Nabbs, are strikingly similar in their activities to the West Riding clothier, John Pawson, who died in 1576.[1] Heaton considers him to be a member of the 'upper middle-class of his fraternity'. Although he too only possessed one loom, he carried out all processes of cloth manufacture except fulling; he even dyed the wool before weaving it. Pawson too could afford to buy large stocks of raw materials in bulk, and had sixty-one stones of wool in stock valued at about £30. He also had cloth worth £31 in his house.

This is the characteristic which probably helps to place Lancashire clothiers such as Nabbs and the others, on a higher level than the 'meaner' clothiers. Unlike Walwork and Butterworth, they were not in a hurry to sell each piece of cloth immediately it was finished in order to buy food or pay for the raw materials which had gone into the making of that cloth. They seem to have been able to work for several months, allowing the cloth to pile up at home, and even when they did eventually sell it, it was usual to allow credit to the men who bought it.

There was another class of woollen clothier in Lancashire on a higher level than these men, although they were few in number even at the end of the sixteenth century. They had managed to expand their business and employed perhaps a dozen people altogether who worked full time in the clothier's own house. A cloth producer of this class would use such large quantities of wool that many spinners and carders would have to be resorted to, in addition to those at work in the house. Consequently the wealth of these upper-class clothiers was substantial; whereas a middle-class weaver would do well to be worth £120, an upper-class man would usually be worth over £250. Again, however, there was no rigid division between the classes.

The best example of a prosperous upper-class clothier was George Holt of Salford, whose total wealth, including debts due to him at his death in 1598, was £329. He lived in a large house which contained a special 'work house', where all the processes of cloth manufacture except fulling, were carried out. The work house contained three pairs of hand cards, three pairs of stock cards, three spinning wheels, three looms, a shear-board and several pairs of shears. This represents quite a step forward in industrial organisation, since, assuming that all Holt's equipment was being used continually, at least fifteen people must have been employed under the one roof—six carding wool, three spinning, three weaving, and

[1] Heaton, op. cit., pp. 97–8.

at least three shearing the cloth. It is unlikely that all these were members of his own family. The amounts of cloth in his warehouse suggest that the equipment was being used full time in the production of rugs and friezes. There was some cloth at the fulling mill, and some had been sent to other parts of the country to be sold. The whole lot is grouped under one heading. There were thirty-seven friezes each worth 27s, twenty-two rugs at 21s. each, and one white rug worth 30s. The total value of the cloth was £72 11s. In the warehouse there were pack cloths and ropes for wrapping up the rest of the cloth when it was sent away to be sold.

Large stocks of wool were needed to keep the business running smoothly, and Holt could afford to keep them on hand. In another room known as the 'further chamber', were almost a hundred and fifty stones of wool, of which a third was Irish wool, the whole stock being worth about £36.

His will is followed by a list of debts owing to him, amounting to not quite £100, but unfortunately not one of them is specified. It is reasonable to assume that some of them were for cloth already sold. For instance, there is £7 due from John Moss of Cambridge, a common market for all types of Lancashire cloth. This debt is almost certainly for cloth, because the previous year the same man bought linen cloth from a Wigan linen draper.[1] It has been suggested[2] that some of these debts were for wool which Holt had supplied to other weavers. There is in fact a group of people who owed him comparatively small sums ranging from only 1s. in some cases to the largest in the group, which was 18s. The same writer goes further and suggests that Holt operated a fully-fledged putting-out system rather like that in Wiltshire where poor weavers had been reduced to the position of mere employees of wealthy clothiers, living a hand-to-mouth existence on the meagre wages of the clothier.[3] It is claimed that four of Holt's debtors who owed large sums of money ranging from £10 to £27 were his agents who organised the delivery of wool and yarn and the collection of cloth in the localities. But this seems doubtful, in view of several objections which can be made. In the first place, the only reason for singling out these four people as agents seems to be that they happened to owe more than the other debtors, which proves nothing. There were four other men who owed sums ranging between £3 6s. 8d. and £7; so could not all eight debts be for wool bought outright from Holt, or, much more likely, for cloth sold by him, remembering that the £7 debt was that owed by the Cambridge man?

As well as this, it is clear that, even if the commodity involved in some of the cases was wool or yarn, the ownership of the materials changed when the debtors handed over the money in return. If these people had

---

[1] infra, ch. v, p. 58.

[2] J. J. Bagley, 'Matthew Markland, a Wigan Mercer; the Manufacture and Sale of Lancashire Textiles in the Reigns of Elizabeth I and James I,' *Lancashire and Cheshire Antiquarian Society*, vol. LXVIII, 1958, pp. 67-8.   [3] Ramsay, op. cit., p. 14 passim.

simply delivered yarn and collected the cloth in the localities, there would have been no exchange of money because Holt would still have been the owner and would have remained the owner even after the cloth was woven. The only money to exchange hands would have been the wages paid by Holt to both agents and weavers. Even the people who owed only a few shillings can be said to have owned the wool. So long as money continued to flow from the other people to Holt, they were independent; it was only when the money passed in the opposite direction in the form of wages, that Holt could be said to operate a putting-out system.

In addition to this there is another objection to the theory. If large numbers of weavers returned cloth to Holt, one would expect him to have had much more cloth in stock than his £72 worth, which was a reasonable amount for a clothier manufacturing with three looms. After all, Pawson, the Yorkshireman, had cloth worth over £30 in his house, and he only had one loom.[1] It is not even certain that Holt ever sold wool. His stock may seem large, but in fact a hundred and fifty stones is not excessive for a clothier with three looms to keep fully supplied. Referring to Pawson again, he had one loom, yet he had sixty-one stones of wool, while John Nabbs had a hundred and eighty stones.

The evidence therefore, is not conclusive that Holt worked a putting-out system. He was a highly successful employer of labour on a small scale, but no more than that, and had probably expanded his business to the maximum size that was desirable. Any larger unit would have become inconvenient and unwieldy, for the size of his house. It had taken him at least seventeen years to evolve his organisation, since he started business as a clothier about 1581. Another Manchester clothier complained to the Court of Exchequer[2] that Holt had not been legally apprenticed to the trade for seven years, but this had obviously not deterred him.

Before turning to consider another clothier it is interesting to notice that even such a large-scale producer as Holt still found time for agriculture. He had two ploughs, four cows and a horse. The crops in his barn—oats, barley and hay—were worth £7; and a picturesque note— he kept a hive of bees in his back garden.

There do not seem to have been many men like Holt in Manchester, but he was not entirely alone. At least two others deserve to be mentioned along with him as upper-class clothiers. First of all there was John Robinson of Strangeways, Salford, who died in 1587. His inventory is less detailed than Holt's, but it tells enough to show that the scales of wealth of both men were remarkably similar. The total value of Robinson's goods and money was just over £330. He had a stock of a hundred and forty-two stones of wool and yarn valued at over £36, and friezes worth almost

[1] See infra, pp. 41–2, Lawrence Robinson, clothier, who bought up large amounts of cloth as well as producing some himself on two looms. He had cloth worth over £500.

[2] E1593/81. Mich. 23 Eliz. Rot. 108, 109.

£70. Some of this cloth was in London awaiting sale, and four of the packs of friezes had already been sold to a merchant called Ralph Seal who had not paid the £29 due for them. This incident provides a good illustration of the risks which a clothier had to take when he allowed credit to merchants who bought his cloth. It was 1587 when the fighting on the continent had seriously hindered the cloth trade, and Seal had been unable to find a buyer for the four packs of friezes at Stourbridge Fair. Until he did so, Robinson would presumably have to wait patiently for his £29. Like Holt, Robinson kept three looms and finished his cloth— he owned three pairs of shears and a shearboard; but he does not seem to have employed carders or spinners in his house.

The other Manchester clothier of the upper class worked on a somewhat smaller scale. He was Francis Hough who died in 1593. He manufactured rugs and friezes, using two looms, and then sheared the cloth, but does not seem to have done any carding or spinning at home. He had a very large stock of wool and flocks valued at over £80, which suggests that Hough may have acted as a wool dealer. There are six debts due to him totalling £12 15s., although the inventory does not state specifically what they were for. The amount of friezes and rugs in his house was relatively small—worth about £10—so there is no possibility of his operating a putting-out system, even if he did sell wool. In addition to cloth manufacture, Hough also leased a field at a rent of £3 a year, and kept in it two cows and three horses. The total value of all his goods and money was £247 19s.

The presence of woollen clothiers outside the Manchester district, comparable in wealth with these Manchester men, was very rare, but they did exist, with the difference that their agricultural activities were much more extensive, and their animals and crops made up a more significant proportion of their wealth. Undoubtedly one of the most prosperous clothiers outside Manchester was Nicholas Halstead of Padiham, near Burnley. Yet even at the end of his life in 1587 he called himself a yeoman rather than a clothier. He produced woollen cloth on two looms and had a large stock of fifty-three stones of wool worth £18 11s. He also had wool spun into yarn valued at £12 6s. 8d. There was raw cloth in the house worth £57 3s. 4d. Although Halstead kept one spinning wheel, wool cards, combs and combstocks for the early processes of cloth manufacture, he did not shear the cloth at home. It seems likely that he sold large amounts of cloth to one man, Thomas Laine, who owed him £182. There were no other debts to speak of. The total value of his possessions is not stated, but appears to be somewhere in the region of £400. Much of this was in leases of land, in crops and in animals. His cattle, horses and pigs for instance, were worth £56, and he kept some twenty sheep valued at £2 10s., which supplied him with a very small proportion of his raw materials.

Lawrence Blakey of Blacko-in-Pendle, who died in 1573 and was buried in Colne Parish Church, was another clothier who kept sheep. They were valued at £11, and must have numbered about a hundred. Blakey was a moderately rich man worth about £200. A larger percentage of the total lay in livestock and crops than in textiles. Yet he was still, in his day, one of the most considerable clothiers of the Colne area. He called himself a clothier in his will, although he owned more animals than Halstead who preferred to think of himself as a yeoman farmer. He owned three looms and had wool and cloth valued at £38, but does not seem to have carried out any other process except weaving. On the other hand he kept ten oxen, eighteen cows, some calves and three horses, which, together with the sheep were worth over £70. Meal and corn amounted to £24.

The cloth was by no means finished when it had been woven. There were two important processes still to be carried out—fulling and shearing. There was also another process which has been touched upon, that of dyeing, which could be done either before or after weaving. In Lancashire it seems to have been more common to dye the raw materials. Several Manchester clothiers had wool already dyed—black, grey, blue, 'straw-colour', and many other shades,[1] before it was spun into yarn. The Shuttleworths of Gawthorpe Hall often had yarn dyed black or blue, although on occasions they had the woven piece dyed.[2]

Less information seems to have survived about dyers than about any other class of clothworker; though it is quite clear that there was in existence a class of independent workers who specialised in dyeing wool and cloth, and charged fixed rates. One Manchester dyer was Humphrey Taplow who was active in the second half of the sixteenth century.[3] Thomas Wignall was a dyer in Liverpool in 1578.[4] William Abbott of Blackburn called himself a dyer in his will drafted in 1591, and seems to have made a prosperous living from the occupation. Though no inventory has survived, the will is followed by a long list of debts owing to him, amounting to over £150. At least six of the debtors living in Blackburn and the surrounding hamlets were engaged in the cloth industry.[5] Their debts range from 4d. to £2 16s. 2d. and were presumably for wool or cloth dyed by Abbott.

On the other hand, some clothiers had taken to dyeing their own raw materials and cloth and from there, had probably extended their business to do work for other clothiers. It was convenient for a prosperous clothier to take over as many of the processes of cloth production as possible. John

[1] George Holt and John Leese, for example.
[2] *Shuttleworth Accounts*, i, pp. 39, 110, 125, 225.
[3] E1593/82, Rot. 81.
[4] *Liverpool Town Books*, II, p. 277, ed. J. A. Twemlow.
[5] Alban Lache, Thomas Lache, John Broxopp, weavers; Thomas Baron, John Brandwood, Richard Lounde.

Abbott, probably the brother of William,[1] seems to have begun his career as a weaver. From his weaving alone, he may be classed as a lower middle rank man, owning a loom, shears, tenters, woollen cards and combs, and kersey cloth, wool and yarn worth almost £34. But in addition to this he had a special dye house containing 'dyeing or lytting ware, leads and tubbs', valued at over £23, far in excess of what would be required to dye his own wool. Yet Abbott still called himself a yeoman and his agricultural capital made up about one third of his total wealth. He kept two yoke of oxen alone worth £21, and there were four other young oxen, fifteen cows, three horses, twenty-four sheep, geese and poultry.

John Leese of Manchester called himself a clothworker. He did at least three different jobs. He bought unfinished cloth and sheared it in his workshop where he had six pairs of broad cloth shears. He had another 'shop' in the same house in which he sold small amounts of many different types of cloth: red friezes, white friezes, blue kersey, silver coloured kersey, green kersey, French tawney kersey, and white rugs. And finally, and most important in this context, he had a dyehouse in which stood 'two greate dyinge leades' valued at £5. The dye stuffs in stock were over two hundredweight of madder worth £5 10s., and fifty-six pounds of brazil worth £2 19s. 4d. He probably made a very comfortable living from this variety of occupations, for all his goods and money were worth £224 4s. when he died in 1598.

The men who worked exclusively as dyers could hardly be expected to take kindly to such men as Leese and Abbott, who may have taken away some of their trade. The Manchester dyers made a great fuss to safeguard their interests, and under the leadership of Humphrey Taplow, laid a series of informations against their rivals in the Court of Exchequer.[2] Between 1581 and 1583 Taplow proceeded against three Manchester men, one of whom was John Leese himself, the other two being Adam Oldham and Stephen Hulme. He accused them of 'occupying the art or mystery of the dyers', without having been apprenticed for seven years, as the statute[3] demanded. All three appeared before the court and pleaded 'not guilty', but what the court decided is not clear. Taplow's efforts certainly had no lasting effect in the case of Leese.

The process undergone by woollen cloth immediately after weaving was that of fulling. It was the fuller's job to cleanse and felt the cloth. This was done by treating it with soap and fuller's earth to remove the oil and size, and then beating it. Unlike the dyers, the Lancashire fullers seem to have kept their profession intact, without competition from wealthy clothiers. Fulling was the one process that even the wealthiest clothier

---

[1] William makes several bequests to 'the children of my brother John'.

[2] E159/382, Pasch. 24 Elizabeth Rot. 81; E159/385, Mich. 25 Eliz. Rot. 123; and E159/384. Pasch. 25 Eliz. Rot. 110.

[3] 5 Elizabeth, cap. 4.

was unable to carry out under his own roof, because the cloth had to be pounded under heavy, water-driven hammers, as it lay in a trough, which could only be done at a fulling mill. No Lancashire clothier owned a fulling mill, although it was not unknown for Wiltshire clothiers to own one.[1] In Lancashire, the owner of a fulling mill did not normally operate the machinery. One mill in Wigan was the property of the parsons of Wigan Parish Church. In 1574 the mill was leased to two men who operated it.[2] A fulling mill in Middleton was owned by Richard Ashton Esquire, who in 1591 leased it out to Ambrose Jackson, 'for a term of lives'. Jackson let the mill to an undertenant, Edward Heywood. It was Heywood who operated the mill 'and did and still dothe take peces and clothes to be mylled and dressed therein'.[3]

In a situation of this sort, complications could arise if anything went wrong during the fulling process. Customers were not sure who was responsible for the cloth left to be fulled, whether it was Jackson or the sub-tenant. In 1600, for instance, Giles Edge brought six packs of cottons to the mill for fulling, but because of negligence on the part of Heywood, the cottons were spoiled and 'the cullor thereof lost'. The owner of the cottons brought a lawsuit against Jackson in the Duchy Court, demanding compensation. Jackson replied that he took no part in working the mill and that it was Heywood who should pay the compensation. There is no mention of the verdict.

Fullers charged fixed rates per piece. One Manchester fuller was Thomas Gorelt, whose fee was 6d. He did extensive business with a Manchester 'cottonman', James Rillston. Just before the latter's death in 1578, Gorelt had fulled a hundred and eighty-eight pieces of cottons at a charge of £4 16s., of which Rillston had already paid £4, and 'the reste I owe him is apparente in my debte booke'. Rillston had also sold Gorelt a horse for £2 18s. 6d., part of which the fuller paid in cash, and the remaining 27s. 6d. he paid by fulling fifty-five pieces of cottons.

The names of several other fullers have survived. Robert and William Bowker, William Wardleworth and Roger Nayden of Bury all did business with Anthony Mosley, a wealthy Manchester clothier who died in 1607.[4] It seems that the occupation was carried on through several generations, as long as the lease or sub-lease held. Both Wardleworth and Nayden had followed in their father's footsteps and the inventories of the two elder men show that the typical Lancashire fuller was a fairly prosperous member of the community. The elder Roger Nayden who died in 1593 had possessions worth about £70. He was able to afford beds and bedding worth £10; his pewter, brass and other furniture were valued at almost £10. Probably for use on military service, he kept a sword, a dagger, a bow and a sheaf of arrows. Like workers in all the other branches of the

---

[1] Ramsay, op. cit., p. 19.   [2] D.L.1/91, F.6.   [3] D.L.1/197, E.6.
[4] infra, p. 68.

industry, his labours at the mill still allowed him time for agriculture. He kept cattle, horses, and pigs valued at £16 6s. 8d., and ploughs, harrows, and carts; he held tacks of ground valued at £12, and had corn and hay on the premises worth £4 13s. 4d. The elder William Wardleworth who died in the previous year, 1592, was in similar circumstances, owning goods, including livestock, worth £108.

Another Wardleworth, Richard, was a fuller at Bury, who not only fulled cloth belonging to other clothiers, but also bought raw cloth probably from small producers, and processed it in his fulling mill. Thus when he died in 1592, he owned six friezes already fulled priced at £1 12s. each, and two unfulled friezes worth £1 10s. each. He was not a wealthy man by any means, being worth slightly over £30.

Some parts of the county were better served by fullers and fulling mills than others. Colne had had a mill at least since 1296 when the Lord of the Manor, Henry de Lacy, insisted that all his tenants in the area should use his newly built mill in the town.[1] At this date the fuller was directly employed by de Lacy who took all the profits. By the early part of the sixteenth century, however, this had changed, and the mill was leased out to tenants at a fixed yearly rent. The tenant in 1527 was Henry Townley.[2] By 1573 something had gone wrong; a number of Colne clothiers complained that 'there neyther nowe is nor of longe time hath beene any good fulling mylles within three or foure myles of the parish of Colne', where they could get their raw kerseys properly fulled. As a result they were forced to take their cloth 'at greate charge', to some fulling mills at Heptonstall in Yorkshire, 'near adjoyning'.[3] In actual fact Heptonstall lies a good ten miles away over the rough country of Boulsworth and Widdop Moors, though admittedly it lay on the well-trodden route between Colne and Halifax.

The next and final stages through which woollen cloth had to pass were the various finishing or dressing processes, of which the main part was the shearing of the cloth. First of all the nap of the cloth was raised with teasels, and then clipped with heavy hand shears so that all the projecting fibres were of equal length. Some cloth manufacturers, as we have already seen, had their cloth dressed at home and kept shearboards and pairs of shears. George Holt, John Robinson, John Nabbs, and Alban Lache, the Blackburn clothier, all kept shears and carried out every process except fulling. Many weavers, however, especially the poorer men, sold their cloth unfinished and sometimes unfulled, to a merchant who arranged for the cloth to be fulled and then had it sheared at his own house, before he sent it away for sale. These men, like others in the industry, tend to confuse matters by calling themselves clothiers; but they did not weave cloth: they only saw to its fulling and dressing. William Baguley was a

[1] W. Bennett, *History of Marsden and Nelson*, p. 32.
[2] *C.C.R.*, ii, p. 381.   [3] D.L.1/83, L.6.

Manchester clothier of this type, who died in 1572. He bought up large quantities of cottons from small producers and had them sheared and finished in his workhouse at home. He owned four pairs of shearman's shears and almost certainly employed men full time on the finishing of cloth which was his own property.

On the other hand there was still a group of independent shearmen, even in Manchester, who took in other men's cloth and charged fixed rates for the shearing of it, in the same way as the independent fullers and dyers did. Richard Rycroft of Colne was a wealthy clothier who had some of his cloth sheared by John Shackleton. When Rycroft died in 1595 he had noted in his will that he still owed Shackleton £9 for dressing cloth.

A shearman could be quite poor, like William Allofield, a Manchester shearman who died of the plague in 1606. An inventory of his goods shows only the barest necessities of life, and his pair of shears.[1] Francis Travis of Oldham, described as a shearman in his will of 1597 was more successful. He owned three pairs of shears, of which he used one himself, and the others were in the hands of two men who were evidently his employees, perhaps apprentices. One of the pairs of shears, kept by Robert College, was described as 'yarde broade cloth shears . . . having a marke of the cross keys upon them'. There were several debts of a few shillings each owing to Travis, probably by the people whose cloth he had sheared. He was prosperous enough to be able to afford a feather-bed and bolster, although his possessions were not worth much more than £20 altogether.

There was a great deal of friction between the independent shearmen and the rich clothiers of the Baguley type, who had cloth sheared by their own employees. The shearmen objected strongly, the dispute coming to a head in 1595 when the shearmen of Manchester and Salford, under the leadership of Ralph Sorocould, sent a petition to the Privy Council. They demanded 'the cottoninge of all suche cottons, rugges and fryzes, as are used to bee within the County Palatine of Lancaster'. The Council decided in favour of the shearmen and ordered that

no trader useinge to buy clothe within the saiede county . . . shall . . . shere, or cottone the same within his owne howse or elsewhere, eyther by himselve or any other by his procurement, but shall cause the same to be rowed, shorne, and cottoned, by suche shermen . . . as shall bee thought fitt and woorthee to have the doinge thereof, in respect of theire good woorkmanship.[2]

On the surface therefore, the shearmen had won the battle, but whether they were completely successful seems doubtful. John Leese[3] for instance, kept six pairs of shears which he used to dress cloth in his own house in 1598, not long after the Privy Council Order. He did not own any looms

---

[1] *Chetham Miscellanies*, 3, p. 16, Chetham Society, New Series, vol. 73, 1915; ed. E. Axon.
[2] Tawney and Power, op. cit., i, pp. 223–5.
[3] *supra*, p. 36.

D

and must therefore have bought the cloth he was dressing, thereby breaking the Privy Council's regulation.

These clothiers who bought cloth from small manufacturers were the wealthiest men in the woollen industry. Their existence proves that there was no widespread putting-out system in operation in Lancashire, because so many of them do not seem to have handled raw materials. It is beyond doubt therefore that small weavers dealt with two different persons: one for the supply of raw materials, the other for the disposal of the cloth. Consider William Baguley; the total valuation of his goods and money was £422 17s. 6d., of which very nearly two thirds were in cottons. There were fifteen packs at home and another fifteen packs had been sent to London, their total value being £262 10s. Yet he too indulged in some agriculture: he owned two fields on lease, valued at £27 10s., where he kept five cows, a calf and a pig, and grew barley and oats. He had over £38 in gold and money in the house when he died. He had no dealings whatsoever with raw materials.

James Rillston who died in 1578, had a similar business, but on a somewhat smaller scale. He called himself a 'cottonman' and after the cloth had been finished off, he took or sent it to London where he had recently sold cottons worth just over £92. Other clothiers of this type whose activities can be glimpsed only momentarily, were Robert Chadwick of Rochdale and Lawrence Fogg, who bought unfinished cottons from Robert Ravald in 1578; and Henry Robinson of Old Land, near Burnley, who bought cloth from weavers in Colne and Great Harwood in the early 1590's.[1]

By far the wealthiest member of this group of clothiers was Anthony Mosley of Manchester, whose career began in the 1580's. When he died in 1607 he owned black, grey and white woollens worth about £500. Some of these were in his warehouse at home, while the rest were in the hands of four fullers.[2] His goods and money were worth well over £2,000 altogether. It must be emphasised that Mosley confined himself strictly to finishing and marketing cloth, much of which was sent to London to his brother Nicholas. There is no trace whatsoever either in the will or the inventory of his dealing in raw materials of any sort.

Some Lancashire clothiers, however, did deal in both finished cloth and raw materials, which raises again the question of the independence of the smaller producers with whom they came into contact. James Chetham of Manchester, for instance, who died in 1575,[3] had sold small quantities of yarn to five men. George Batersby of Bury owed him 4s.; Morris Prestwich of Hulme owed £1, the largest debt. At the other end of the textile industry Chetham had supplied cottons to merchants in Hull and Chester,

---

[1] *supra*, pp. 30–1.   [2] *supra*, p. 37.
[3] E. A. Axon, *Chetham Genealogies*, pp. 38–41; Chetham Society, New Series, vol. 50, 1903.

who still owed him a total of £19 12s. However, this is very small-scale business when compared with Baguley's activities and with those of some of the Lancashire linen yarn dealers.[1] The debts for raw materials are not listed neatly in a businesslike fashion, but are scattered at random among other items such as this pleasant one: 'Mr. John Chetam of Nutterst for iiij trees as yett standinge, the price of every tree is ixs. vid.' This scarcely suggests a highly organised capitalist system. Nor is there anything to suggest that the weavers were under any obligation to return the cloth to Chetham.

John Wolstencroft of Bury who died in 1588, called himself a clothier, and had some dealings in wool. These were not his primary concerns, however, for the wool in stock was valued at no more than £4 10s. On the other hand he had cloth worth £43 and some sets of tenterbars. There was really no question of his operating a putting-out system, since he actually bought the cloth from small producers. In fact he still owed one weaver, Ralph Buckley, 20s. for a piece of black woollen cloth.

Another Manchester clothier who deserves mention is Lawrence Robinson, who died in 1587, one of the wealthiest clothiers in the county. His activities differed from those of other clothiers in that he not only bought up and finished woollen cloth, but also produced large amounts in his own house. In his 'worke chamber' were a shearboard and two pairs of shears. These would not be enough to process the large amounts of cloth with which he dealt, so that many other shearmen as well as fullers must have been kept busy by Robinson. He also kept two looms in a special loom house, where rugs were produced. There were twenty pieces of rugs worth about £17 which had been woven in the house, and one piece bought elsewhere. Robinson also owned cottons and Rochdale friezes worth £446 12s., some of which were in his house and some at the fulling mills. Other cloth worth over £32 was in London waiting to be sold, and he had already sold some cloth for which two merchants owed him a total of £35 10s. The amount of raw wool in stock was surprisingly small, worth only £3 8s. 8d., and there is no evidence that he sold wool to other weavers. A surprising fact was that he had three packs of Irish linen yarn valued at £42 10s., though there was no sign of linen cloth.[2] This wide variety of activity brought him a substantial income. He lived in a large comfortable house of at least ten rooms, and had feather beds and bedding alone worth £26. He owned some land and kept four cows and a horse. In the house was the extraordinarily large sum of £720 in money, gold and silver, and although no figure is mentioned, his total wealth was not far short of £2000.

The men who carried out similar functions in other parts of Lancashire were much less wealthy. One clothier who bought and sold cloth as well as manufacturing some himself was Richard Rycroft of Colne, who died

---

[1] infra, ch. iv.   [2] See infra, ch. vii, pp. 97–8, for a discussion of this point.

in 1595. He owned two looms, together with cards and combs, and had a stock of wool worth £3. There was no cloth in the house, but three London merchants owed him a total of £98. He himself owed £9 to John Shackleton for dressing of cloth and he owed over £100 to forty-seven other people from whom he had presumably bought cloth. Two of these men, Henry Shaw whom he owed 15s., and William Holt, £10, were both prosperous weavers, as their inventories show. In spite of handling such large amounts of cloth, Rycroft's way of life remained modest. All his possessions were worth about £40, and when all his debts were paid he would be worth something like £140. He still called himself a yeoman, and held a field on a thirty years' lease, worth annually £10.

When it had been dressed, woollen cloth was completed, and ready to be sold. At that point a piece of cloth might be owned by one of three different types of person. It might still be the property of a poor weaver who had employed the services of a shearman for its final dressing; this was apparently not very common. It might be owned by one of the middle- or upper-class weavers who sheared and completed their own cloth at home. Or the cloth might already have changed owners once and be the property of a rich clothier such as Baguley who specialised in finishing and marketing cloth bought from lots of poor weavers. But this is now straying on to the subject of a later chapter.

This survey of the Lancashire woollen industry thus reveals an organis-ation composed chiefly of small-scale workers; but wills and inventories probably do not tell the whole story. The slightly frustrating truth is that it is not possible to examine in detail the circumstances of the poorest independent weavers and other clothworkers nor those who were employed by other clothiers. The poorest woollen weaver whose will has survived was Edward Butterworth, the Rochdale man who died in 1598, worth less than £17. Yet there must have been some in greater poverty than this—some linen weavers were poorer[1]—men who were unable to afford the writing of a will. When a man such as George Holt appears on the scene, who employed perhaps fifteen people in his own house, and when one finds shearmen and dyers protesting because other and richer clothiers were taking over their jobs, then it is clear that the organisation of the woollen industry was showing many signs, by the late 1590's, of moving towards the kind of system in which capitalist employers, while in no way dominating the industry, were becoming more numerous. The reasons as to why some men had come to be employed by others are not entirely clear. Whether they had once been independent and had then been forced by uncertainty of markets to succumb to the capitalist, is impossible to tell. What can be concluded with certainty is that these de-velopments towards a capitalistically controlled industry were in their very earliest stages in 1600, and were probably confined to the Manchester area.

[1] *infra*, ch. iv, p. 46.

CHAPTER IV

THE ORGANISATION OF THE
LINEN INDUSTRY

NOTHING has been written so far about the organisation of the second important branch of the Lancashire textile industry, the manufacture of linen cloth. In the past the importance of the linen industry has sometimes been underestimated. One writer[1] even claimed that there was no linen industry worth mentioning either in Lancashire or Cheshire, in the sixteenth century. In fact, in the area around Manchester there was a highly developed industry in operation which rivalled woollen manufacture in importance. Liverpool and Ormskirk, which had no woollen industry to speak of, were also centres of linen manufacture, and so were Bolton, Blackburn, Preston, Burnley and Wigan. On the other hand, linen manufacture seems scarcely to have existed in Bury, Rochdale and Colne.

It can be stated at once that the organisation of the linen industry was similar to that of the woollens. The work was done mostly by poor but independent weavers who bought raw materials on credit, but were free to dispose of their handiwork wherever possible. As in the case of the woollen workers there were many differing scales of wealth, and some linen weavers were highly prosperous.

The processes involved in preparing flax for weaving were quite complicated. The flax was pulled in the field before it was fully ripe, after which it was immersed in water and left to soak for as long as twelve days in order to rot the outer woody part of the stem so that it could be easily removed from the fibre. During the earlier decades of the sixteenth century, this soaking had usually been done in rivers, streams and ponds, and produced a most unpleasant stench, as well as fouling the water so that it was unfit for cattle to drink. It was for these reasons that in 1541 the government prohibited the soaking of flax in water which had to serve cattle.[2]

The next stage in the process was to dry the flax out over a fire burning over a hole or gig dug in the ground. This could be done inside a house

[1] Longfield, op. cit., p. 156.
[2] 33 Henry VIII, cap. 17.

provided it was equipped with a properly built kiln. Without this there was the danger that the flax might catch fire and cause a serious outbreak. It was to avoid this that in 1540 the Liverpool Town Council ordered that no drying of flax or hemp must take place inside a house.[1] Anybody who disobeyed the order was to be fined 3s. 4d. The order was extended in 1572 to include the drying of flax within six roods of a house if there was any danger of the house being set on fire,[2] the following year the distance was increased to eight roods,[3] and to ten in 1575.[4] This did not prevent people from continuing to dry their flax and no doubt many managed to avoid being found out. Some were not so fortunate, however, for in the years following, nine people were fined for breaking the order.[5] In 1591 the Town Council found it necessary to repeat the order,[6] but even so it probably had little effect. A widow Abraham was fined 2s. 6d. in 1597 for gigging flax in her kitchen and therefore causing danger of fire.[7]

When the flax was dry it was beaten to separate the fibre from the outer part of the stem. This process together with the drying was known as 'gigging'. The fibre was then combed or carded out into long strands and spun into a continuous thread. At this point the linen yarn required bleaching. Sometimes in fact, the flax was laid out to be bleached before it was spun into yarn, but the main bleaching time was during the yarn stage. The 1542 Act[8] which removed the sanctuary from Manchester to Chester to prevent the yarn being stolen as it lay bleaching, stated that yarn had to 'lye withoute aswell in the nyght as in the day contynually, for the space of one half yere to be whyted before it can be made cloth'.

The early processes of soaking, gigging, carding and spinning could be done by women, as is shown by the fact that half the people fined in Liverpool for illegal gigging of flax and hemp were women. At Samlesbury in the Ribble Valley, the Court Leet found it necessary to regulate the activities of spinners.[9] It is clear from the regulation that the process was mainly carried out by women: 'We are Agryed that no women shall goe Abroade into theire neighbours howses with theire distaves, nether daye nor night, nor spyne by the waye, for ev'y tyme so doinge the spynner shall forfete and paye xiid.' Exactly what the Court Leet was hoping to achieve by this regulation is not clear, but one can only suppose that they aimed to prevent thefts of yarn which were certainly common and were usually committed by women. The Lancashire Quarter Sessions Records contain more than one instance of a woman stealing her neighbours' yarn.[10]

[1] *Liverpool Town Books*, I, p. 9.   [2] ibid., II, p. 52.   [3] ibid., II, p. 128.
[4] ibid., II, p. 211.
[5] ibid., II, pp. 52, 160, 264, 304, 423, 507, 555.   [6] ibid., II, p. 611.
[7] ibid., II, p. 740.   [8] 33 Henry VIII, cap. 15.
[9] J. Croston, *History of the Ancient Hall of Samlesbury*, p. 99.
[10] *Lancashire Quarter Sessions Records*, ed. J. Tait, i, 1590–1606, pp. 84, 78, 99, 286; Chetham Society, New Series, vol. 77, 1917.

A good example of a family who prepared flax into yarn and then sold it to a weaver, is that of Richard Hunter of Bickerstaff in the parish of Ormskirk who kept two spinning wheels and a pair of cards. He had hemp, flax and tow worth £2 3s. 4d. and three slippings of yarn worth a shilling. But this was as far as he went with linen manufacture. He did not own a loom and still looked upon himself as a husbandman. When he died in 1582, his animals and husbandry gear made up about three quarters of his total wealth which amounted to £32 5s. 1d.

The length of the bleaching process which the yarn had to undergo before it could be woven, created problems for the weaver. If he bought unbleached yarn he could expect to have a six months' wait before he could begin work on it. Many of the poorer weavers could not afford to wait so long before turning the yarn into money, unless the yarn dealer allowed them a very long period of credit. Thus a separate class of worker developed who specialised in bleaching linen yarn. The hamlet of Moston, outside Manchester, was a centre for yarn bleaching; in 1595 it was explained by its inhabitants, with some exaggeration, that this was their only source of income, and that they needed turf from the waste land around the hamlet, for fuel; for the bleaching of linen yarn 'doth requyre very moche fyre'.[1]

These Moston men probably drew some of their livelihood from agriculture, and it seems likely that bleachers of linen yarn would have to be men with a sound agricultural backing which would allow them to exist through the long periods during which they were waiting for yarn to bleach. Thomas Bamford, a prosperous Manchester yeoman farmer with cattle, horses, and crops worth almost £50, was a good example of this class of worker. He bought and bleached linen yarn, and when he died in 1602 he owned linen yarn worth £7 2s. of which almost half was described as being 'at the whiting'. He had a hut set aside for fuel and this contained ten shillings worth of turf. But he did no weaving and had no dealings in finished cloth. The values stated in his inventory for the different sorts of linen yarn give some idea of how much profit could be made from bleaching. The figures seem to suggest that the finest linen yarn very nearly trebled its value when it was bleached. The prices in this instance were 1s. 2d. a pound before, and 3s. a pound after, bleaching.

However, there was no hard and fast rule about yarn bleaching. There was a wide variety of practices and not all the yarn was bleached by men such as these. Many weavers were allowed long credit by the yarn dealer and carried out their own bleaching. Some, especially around Blackburn, carried out all the processes, having bought their yarn in the flax or hemp stage,[2] although this was comparatively rare in the Manchester area, which was principally supplied from Ireland with fully prepared yarn.

[1] Wadsworth and Mann, p. 28.
[2] infra, pp. 50–1.

And inevitably some yarn dealers themselves took over the bleaching process.[1] This class of middlemen on which hundreds of small weavers depended, will be examined in detail later. Firstly, however, to consider examples of the poorer linen weavers.

It is possible to quote several examples of very poor weavers who, perhaps rather surprisingly, were able to afford the writing of a will. The first of these was Humphrey Davis of Barton-on-Irwell, near Manchester, who had himself described as a linen weaver when his will was written in 1594. The sum total of all his possessions was exactly £8 15s. 2d. His loom was worth two shillings, his spinning wheel five shillings, and a small stock of hemp, a coarser fibre than flax, used for the cheapest kind of linen cloth, was valued at three shillings. But at least he owned this equipment in spite of his poverty. His most valuable assets were barley, oats and hay which were worth £2 16s. He also kept two cows and some poultry. The furniture in his house was primitive, to say the least: 'Bords, cheres, stooles, and Bedstockes' were valued at 2s. 6d., bedding at 11s., pewter and brass at 1s. 8d., and finally 'bodie apparell' at 8s.

Another linen weaver of similar poverty was John Turnough of Oldham who died in 1592, and whose total wealth amounted to £8 15s. 1d. There was one unusual point about Turnough: he had no agricultural activities whatsoever. But again, though he was certainly poor, he was independent, because he owned the linen cloth he had made, which was valued at £4 6s. 8d. This, together with his loom, healds and reeds worth £1 8s., made up almost two thirds of his total wealth.

There was also John Pycroft who lived in Manchester itself and died in 1590, worth about £14. He was a linen weaver who kept his loom in a special 'loom house'. He requested that his 'looming neighbours', John Clough and Ralph Shalcross, should see that his will was carried out. His inventory is of special interest because it lists in minute detail the contents of his house, and gives a very full picture of the living conditions of these poor weavers. The furniture consisted of six chairs and four stools, seven cushions, arks and boards. Their total value was precisely 8s. 3d. Next in the list were his pewter vessels mentioned by weight: thirty-six pounds at 6d. a pound, and another sixteen pounds at 4d. a pound. Five metal pots weighed forty-four pounds altogether and were valued at 4d. a pound. Then came a frying-pan, fire irons, a shovel, a pair of tongs, two axes and two candlesticks. For a poor man, Pycroft was comfortably off as far as beds and bedding were concerned. He had one bed and two mattresses, a pair of flaxen sheets and three pairs of hempen sheets, perhaps of his own weaving, six blankets, three bolsters and five pillows. To complete the household picture, the inventory mentions 'odd wood and two ladders' worth 2s., 'seven foot of glass' at 2s. 4d., and finally 'mucke and dunge in the yarde', 8d.

[1] Wadsworth and Mann, p. 11.

Slightly better off than these three weavers were men like Thomas Gill of Bickerstaff, Ormskirk, who kept a loom and its equipment and had a stock of hemp, flax and yarn worth 17s., but who relied far less on weaving for a comfortable livelihood than did the two weavers just mentioned. Gill's main source of wealth seems to have been agriculture. He still looked on himself as a husbandman until his death in 1593. He owned a yoke of bullocks, a cow, a calf, a heifer, and 'two olde mayors', worth over £7, and oats, barley and rye worth £4 8s. With all these and his carts and plough, his agricultural capital was worth £13 11s. 8d. out of a total of approximately £17 10s.

Richard Wilkinson of Hulme, one of the hamlets near Manchester, stood a little higher yet in the scale of wealth, being worth about £28. He kept a loom and had linen yarn worth £2, but he also made some money from selling crops. Just before his death in 1598 he had sold small quantities of barley. Richard Osbaldeston of Billington near Blackburn, still looked on himself as a husbandman in spite of his weaving activities. He had a special workhouse where he kept his loom and his raw materials. Some of this at least was bought in the raw stage, and there was hemp worth 5s. among the stock. He had cards and two spinning wheels with which to convert the hemp into yarn. But he also bought yarn already spun. On one occasion during the year before his death, he had bought four stones of yarn for £1 6s. from a dealer named Thomas Lund, who lived at Clayton-le-Moors, about four miles away. At the time of his death, Osbaldeston's yarn stock was worth £1 8s. 8d., and linen cloth made by him and still unsold was valued at £1.

Large numbers of linen weavers even more prosperous than these were housed in the hamlet of Eccles, near Manchester. A typical example, John Hey, who lived at the Booths, in Eccles and who died in 1597, was worth almost £44, of which £9 13s. 4d. was in yarn 'bothe flaxen and canvas'. His loom, healds and reeds were valued at 14s., so that almost one quarter of his wealth lay in industrial capital. Most of the remainder was in agriculture: he held a 'tacke of grounde' worth £10, and kept three cows and a little calf. One significant possession of his was a small stock of coal, which along with turves, was estimated to be worth £1, and may well have been intended for use in the bleaching of linen yarn.

A weaver of comparable prosperity was William Sandforth who lived in Manchester and kept three looms, though whether all three were used the whole time seems doubtful, otherwise one would have expected him to be worth much more than a modest £50. However, he did have a large stock of white linen yarn worth almost £21, and three pieces of coarse linen cloth called sackcloth, worth £3 10s. Again almost all the rest of his wealth was made up of livestock and crops, and the house was sparsely furnished.

Further north, in Padiham, near Burnley, a great wool producing area, lived Richard Shorrock, who died in 1574. He was a linen weaver whose total wealth amounted to about £44, which included a loom, a spinning wheel, a pair of cards, and yarn worth £19 10s. His sister Ellen did some of the spinning for him, and his will states that he owed her 13s. 4d. for spinning eight stones of yarn.

A neighbour of John Hey at the Booths in Eccles was Giles Roscoe who managed to make more profit out of linen weaving than his neighbour did. His will, dated 1596, calls him a 'linenwebster', and the inventory shows that as well as his loom and its equipment he had a stock of yarn and cloth worth £25, which is about thirty per cent of his total wealth of just over £80.

An Eccles man who began as a linen weaver and later extended his activities to dealing in small quantities of linen yarn, was Richard Lansdale who died in 1588. In his will he had himself described as a yarn buyer although the inventory still refers to him as a linen webster. He kept a loom and two spinning wheels and at his death there was linen cloth worth £1 6s. 8d. in the house. The most valuable single item in his inventory is the stock of linen yarn which was worth £18 11s. 8d. The will contains a list of twelve debts owing to him, totalling £17 7s., and although it is not actually stated, one can assume that they were debts for yarn, because they follow a familiar pattern: for many of the debts a date is given when payment was due to be made. A man named Thurstan Collier owed a pound, due at the Feast of the Purification of the Virgin Mary, and the same man owed a further twenty shillings due on July 27th, 1588. This means that just under half of Lansdale's total wealth of £84 lay in yarn and cloth. He was a substantial farmer too; he kept seven cows, two calves, three horses, two pigs and some poultry. The crops growing on his land were estimated to be worth £5, and there was a stock of hay valued at £2 5s.

The wealthiest linen weavers had capital approaching £200, and they were few in number. Giles Hilton of Oldham belonged to this group. As a substantial yeoman farmer, owning twelve cows and two pigs, he had a certain basic security. His equipment included carts, ploughs and harrows, and the crops in the barn were valued at £17. The total value of all his agricultural stuff including animals was £43. For the manufacture of linen cloth he had at least two looms and when he died in 1592 the linen yarn and cloth in the house were worth £80—almost half his wealth of £176 15s. 4d. Hilton apparently bought most of his raw materials in the form of yarn which he obtained in Manchester. On one occasion in 1590 for instance, he bought linen yarn from an Irishman in Manchester for £26.[1] But in spite of his prosperity, Hilton did not pay cash; he was allowed credit for a short period. The transaction was not completed smoothly, and some months later Hilton found that the Irishman, a Dubliner

[1] Req. 2/110/32.

named Thomas Money or Mooney, had started proceedings against him in the Court of Exchequer, complaining that the money had not been paid. Hilton himself started proceedings against Money in the Court of Requests, complaining that he had paid the £26 but that Money was seeking to take advantage of his 'honeste dealinge', by reason of the fact that the money had been paid in secret with no witnesses present, knowing that Hilton could not prove the payment. Money replied that in the first place the price of the yarn was £28 4s. 9d., not £26, and that secondly the Court of Exchequer had already reached a verdict in his favour. He craved that Requests would uphold that verdict. Whether or not it did is not clear, but Hilton still seems to have been reasonably well off when he died only a few months later, and was certainly not 'impoverished', which he claimed would be the result if the verdict went against him.

Dealers in flax and linen yarn were numerous; thus a linen weaver would be by no means bound to one dealer for his raw materials. In the Manchester area there was great variation in the scale and activity of these dealers. To begin with there were the Irishmen like Thomas Money, who sold whole packs of linen yarn to wealthy weavers or to local dealers who afterwards retailed it in small amounts. Some local dealers were only small men who sold flax and yarn in small quantities along with other goods. John Davie, who died in 1573, kept a shop in Manchester where he had flax valued at £1 13s. 4d. and yarn at £4, together with small amounts of sackcloth, canvas, 'Yorkshire cloth', and kerseys worth £5 10s. His debt book contains a list of thirty-three people who owed him for yarn, flax and cloth. They were mostly for small sums of just a few shillings, and strangely enough, there was one debt of 15s. for some fish.

It seems to have been a common practice for Manchester linen yarn dealers to carry on some other occupation as well. Thomas Brownsword ran a similar sort of business to Davie, though on a rather larger scale. As well as this, he bought small quantities of woollen cloth and sheared it in his shop, where he kept a shearboard and two pairs of shears. When he died in 1588, however, the most valuable items in the shop were flax worth £18 10s., and white linen yarn valued at £2 18s. For weighing the yarn and flax he kept a pair of balances, a beam and a lead weight. There is no mention of any linen cloth in the shop, but woollens—cottons and friezes—were valued at almost £3. Finally there was a small stock of flocks, three stones to be exact, valued at 12s. Brownsword also found time for agriculture, and in fact his cattle and crops were worth £36, more than all the stock in his shop.

Andrew Renshaw, who died in 1591, went about his business in a different way, and concentrated mostly on selling linen yarn, although he spent some of his time making boots and shoes and some farming. At the point when the inventory was taken, he owned two and a half packs of yarn valued at £48 10s. He seems to have employed three men in outlying hamlets to act as agents for the sale of linen yarn. Thus the inventory mentions 'a packe of yarne at John Bexwick's of Blackley'. Another pack was at Francis Hulme's of Blackley, and the remaining half pack with Richard Ogden at Moston. One can only assume that these men either sold the yarn for Renshaw, or that they were bleaching it for him, remembering that Moston was one of the hamlets whose inhabitants specialised in that occupation. It is at least clear that the men did not weave the yarn into cloth and return it to Renshaw, because he had no dealings at all in finished cloth. He also sold yarn directly on credit. John Shawcross had bought half a pack; the price was £10 and it was to be paid on the Feast Day of St. Bartholomew.

When he was not occupied in buying and selling yarn, Renshaw worked as a cobbler. His equipment consisted of boot trees, lasts, a grindstone and other tools worth 6s. 4d; there were whole hides and other pieces of leather valued at £2 16s. The boots and shoes in stock were worth £4. Finally, he held several small pieces of land on which he kept grazing cattle worth over £10. The total value of all his goods and debts amounted to just over £110.

Another Manchester man who combined a number of activities was James Bradshaw, who, when his will was written in 1588, preferred to have himself described as a saddler. Even so he sold linen yarn on a large scale. There was a large stock in the house described as Irish yarn and valued at £20. The will is followed by a long list of debts due to him, presumably for yarn and saddles, but unfortunately only two are specified. Both are for yarn: one of £7 owing by John Bradshaw of Corseybank, and the other of £9 from Thomas Shelmerdine. Bradshaw appeared to have no dealings with linen cloth.

In other areas dealers seem to have confined themselves more to the one occupation. The district around Blackburn provides two excellent examples of how a dealer organised and carried out his business. Firstly, there was John Dewhirst of Clayton-le-Dale, who died in 1592. He dealt extensively in flax which he supplied on credit, usually in small quantities, to large numbers of local spinners and weavers. But he had not extended his activities to buying up finished linen cloth and still had himself described as a husbandman in his will. His inventory is followed by a long and carefully written list headed 'Flax Money', which contains the names of fifty people who owed him for flax. The list mentions the name of the buyer, the amount of flax in stones, and the sum of money owed. Between them the fifty people had bought one hundred and sixty-five stones worth just over £58. The price was invariably 7s. 1d. a stone. The most usual amount to buy was two stones, although one woman, Alice Brown, had bought eleven, for which she owed £3 17s. 11d.

Dewhirst made quite a prosperous living although he was not excessively rich. His house was comfortably furnished, he was able to afford bedding worth almost £8, as well as feather beds, mattresses and bolsters worth three guineas. His agricultural activities must have helped the economy considerably: his farm animals included seventeen cows, five horses and a couple of pigs, worth a total of just over £46. He had in stock barley, wheat, oats, and malt worth nearly £22. The total value of all his possessions, including the debts owing to him was approximately £170.

The other dealer from the Blackburn area, active at the same time as Dewhirst but on a larger scale, was Thomas Lund, who lived at Clayton and died in 1591. He sold linen yarn and also unprocessed hemp. His stock of yarn, some bleached and some unbleached, was valued at slightly over £20, and the hemp was worth £1 6s. 8d. Like Dewhirst's, his inventory is followed by a neat list, or rather in this case two lists of people owing for raw materials. The first list, containing a hundred and twenty debts, is for yarn at prices between 5s. 2d. and 6s. 6d. a stone, which is surprisingly cheap when compared with Dewhirst's price which was for raw flax. The total amount due to him for yarn was about £90. The second list, a much shorter one, contains debts for hemp. There are twenty-two debts for hemp at 4s. a stone, for a total of thirty-seven and a half stones worth £7 10s. The amounts of both yarn and hemp bought by any single person vary between one and seven stones.

What class of person were these men who bought their raw materials a few stones at a time on credit from Lund? It was possible to trace only one of the names on the list, that of Richard Osbaldeston[1] who bought four stones of yarn at 6s. 6d. a stone in 1591. If he is taken as being typical of the others, then it is clear that the Blackburn area contained a thriving linen industry made up of fairly small, but independent and prosperous weavers. Surprisingly, Lund still regarded himself as a husbandman rather than a clothier or even yeoman, since he was a considerable farmer owning cattle worth £40, and oats, barley and hay worth £13.

It is when a dealer became ambitious and began to buy up linen cloth, that the links between producer and middleman became closer, especially if a weaver sold his cloth to the same dealer as had supplied him with raw materials. But it is difficult to fathom the exact relationship in many cases. Edward Holt was a Wigan linen draper who died in 1597. One part of his business was similar to that of Dewhirst and Lund—the supplying of flax to large numbers of weavers on credit. Thirty-five men and women owed him sums ranging from 5s. 8d. to £2 12s. 8d. for flax. The price per stone varied widely and might be anything between 3s. 9d. and 6s. 8d. per stone. The list is even more complete than those of the Blackburn dealers, because as well as giving name, number of stones and price, it mentions the village or hamlet where the debtor lived. There were men in his debt living in Blackrod, Walsh Whittle, Adlington, Anderton, and even as far away as Chorley. And yet the scale of his flax dealing was more

[1] supra, p. 47.

modest than that of the Blackburn men; the total of the debts for flax was no more than £32 14s. 2d.

The main sphere of his activities was in buying up linen cloth from weavers and selling it in large quantities in places as far away as Cambridge and Wellingborough.[1] The huge sum of £755 4s. 9d. was owing to him in this second list, and although not all these debts are stated as being for cloth, there is no other obvious possibility. Even such a busy man as Holt had time for agriculture, keeping nine cows, three stirks, a heifer, four calves and two pigs, worth just over £31. He also owned two ploughs and had grown crops worth £12. His six horses were probably used for carrying cloth. Taking all into consideration, Holt carried on a highly successful business; in fact when all his debts had been paid he would have been worth only a few shillings short of £870, of which probably over eighty per cent was in debts for linen cloth.

Clearly such large amounts of cloth could not have been produced only by the men who bought flax from Holt. He must therefore have bought up cloth from men who had obtained their raw materials elsewhere, which seems to indicate the existence of a fairly free market in which weavers were not bound to one man either for raw materials or for the distribution of the cloth. The weavers with whom Holt himself dealt, seem to have been prosperous enough if the example of Alexander Slater of Walsh Whittle was typical. The debt list shows that he bought two stones of flax at 6s. 4d. a stone from Holt. When he died ten years later he owned a loom, a spinning wheel, flax worth £7 and linen yarn worth £8. His farm animals were valued at just over £20, and he could afford bedding worth £6 5s., a sure sign of prosperity. The value of all his possessions, including a few debts owing to him, was £80 16s. 10d.

John Cocke,[2] a dealer who lived at Cocke Bank, Ashton-under-Lyne, provides a rather different example. Although he was by no means such a wealthy man as Holt—all his possessions and debts amounted to approximately £340—he may have had much closer connections with weavers than Holt did. He sold flax and bought up linen cloth, some of which he sold in the Midlands and south of England. Two women together owed him 22s. 8d. for four stones of flax. His inventory mentions 'yarne to be forty pieces of sackinge, £48; yarn to be six pieces of bolstering, £5 2s.; in cloth woven and at weaving, £48; wares sent into the country, £33'.

Much depends on what interpretation one places on the phrase 'at weaving'. It could be taken to refer to cloth in the process of being manufactured in local households by weavers who were dependent on or employed by Cocke, and which they were bound to return to him, since

---

[1] infra, ch. v, p. 58.

[2] Will and inventory of John Cocke, quoted by W. M. Bowman, *England in Ashton-under-Lyne*, pp. 556–8.

it was still his property.[1] On the other hand, Cocke himself owned two looms complete with gear, so that the cloth may have been 'at weaving' on his own looms. Again, the phrase 'yarne to be forty pieces of sackinge', could indicate that Cocke operated a putting-out system, and that this yarn was intended to be distributed among local weavers and collected after it had been woven. Unfortunately, the list of debts owing to him by local people, and which could well be for flax and yarn, does not mention what commodities were involved; nor was it possible to trace any of the people mentioned, so that the exact nature of Cocke's activities in the linen industry must remain obscure. To complicate matters further, he also bought woollen cloth, chiefly friezes, of which he had sent £24 worth to Bury St. Edmunds to be sold. But he had no dealings with raw wool or woollen yarn. The best that can be said about Cocke's activities is that linen cloth was produced in his house, he sold raw materials on credit, he probably bought linen cloth from other weavers just as he bought woollen cloth, since the amounts involved seem too large to have been produced on his two looms alone; and he may have had some of his yarn woven by men to whom he paid wages. What can be concluded with some certainty is that Cocke's business was an expanding one and represents a step forward on the road towards capitalism. Already he himself must have ceased to play any part in manufacture; much of his time was spent travelling with his nine packhorses to places as far afield as Norwich, Spalding, Northampton, Newport Pagnell, Kettering, Leicester and Dunstable, places which he had visited shortly before his death in 1590 and where he had sold cloth worth about £50, while other members of the family, or perhaps employees from outside the family group, worked at the two looms.

The pattern of a linen manufacturer acting as a yarn dealer and as a buyer of linen cloth from smaller men, was to be found also in Manchester, in the person of Robert Birch, a linen-draper who died in 1583. In his case, however, there was no question of his operating a putting-out system. He owned two looms and when he died he had a stock of raw materials made up of whitened linen yarn worth about £65, and five hundred pounds of flax valued at £9 5s. Cloth in the warehouse, some of it no doubt produced in the house, consisted of thirty-two broad pieces of linen, forty-six pieces of very coarse linen or sackcloth, and three bolster pieces, worth altogether £98 2s. This amount of cloth seems perhaps too large to have been produced wholly by Birch's two looms, and it is this fact which suggests that he probably bought linen cloth from other producers.

The inventory is followed by a remarkable list of debts due to Birch, about a hundred and thirty of them, totalling over £270. The list does not state what the debts are for, only that they appear 'by bills in his

[1] This is the conclusion drawn by Bowman, op. cit., p. 419.

book', but it is safe to assume that some of them at least are for linen yarn or for flax. The reason for this is that every one of the six debtors[1] whom it was possible to trace was either a linen weaver or was connected in some way with the industry. All of them were independent and owned the raw materials in their house, even though Birch allowed them credit.

One of the weavers was William Birch, a comparatively poor husband-man of Heaton Norris who had bought yarn from his namesake for a pound. He owned possessions worth no more than £23 16s. 3d., but he had his own loom, reeds, warp stocks and woods, and a small stock of yarn, all of which were worth £1 4s. 4d. John Derbeshire of Eccles was another of the weavers with whom Birch had dealings. Derbeshire owed him 10s. 1d. At the time of his death some years later he had built up a highly prosperous business; he had possessions worth over £80, owned a loom and had a stock of linen yarn and tow worth £10.

In the dealings of Robert Birch with local weavers, it is clear that the yarn became the property of the weaver who was free to find the best buyer he could for his cloth in the weekly market; that buyer may or may not have been Robert Birch. As for the weaver himself, he would also have a choice of dealers from whom he could buy his raw materials, and need not be bound solely to Birch.

This was in 1583, and although Birch was highly prosperous—the total value of his goods and money amounted to approximately £440—his activities were modest in comparison with those of one or two other extremely wealthy Manchester linen drapers who made small fortunes in the latter part of the sixteenth century, when the linen industry must have undergone a vast expansion. For a short period of perhaps a quarter of a century, while the foreign markets for Lancashire cottons and the woollen trade in general were completely disrupted by the wars, the linen industry, producing cloth for home consumption, provided rich profits, and a number of outstanding drapers were busy in the Manchester area. The Tipping brothers, Richard, Samuel and George, whose father had come to Manchester from Preston,[2] were all occupied in making fortunes in the linen trade. Richard died in 1592, but his wife Isabella continued the business, selling raw materials on credit and buying linen cloth from weavers, for a further six years until her death in 1598. At that time she was worth something in the region of £1500, of which well over half was in linen yarn and cloth. The stock of yarn consisted of white yarn worth about £310 and unbleached or grey yarn worth about £131. The cloth in the warehouse, mostly sackcloth, was worth just over £265. A hundred and forty packs of sackcloth had been sent to London, and these were

---

[1] William Birch of Heaton Norris, (1590); John Derbeshire of Eccles, (1592); Robert Shelmerdine of Levenshulme, (1592); James Bradshaw of Manchester, (1588); Thomas Pollitt of Eccles, (1588); John Riding of Eccles, (1601).

[2] Wadsworth and Mann, p. 29.

valued at £128. The house contained no looms, yet the inventory mentions one significant item: 'sackcloth at weaving'. Actually there was no sackcloth 'at weaving' at the time of Isabella Tipping's death, for the phrase is followed by a blank space. It seems likely therefore, that on occasions she had employed weavers who worked with raw materials which belonged to her. But it also seems that this was not a permanent arrangement, that it was not her chief concern to organise the manufacture of cloth.

Another linen draper active in Manchester in the last decade of the sixteenth century, was Richard Nugent who lived in Salford. The first mention of his name in surviving records was in 1589 when he sold cloth worth £345 in London and Stourbridge.[1] This business was transacted on behalf of his mother-in-law, Elizabeth Goldsmith, who manufactured woollen cloth. Later, however, Nugent developed his own business, and after the death of his wife's parents, specialised in the linen trade until his death in 1609. One aspect of his activities was the selling of linen yarn on credit to hundreds of small weavers. His inventory is followed by two lists of debts, of which the first is headed 'doubtful and desperate', but this contains only three names. The second list is headed 'more in debts by booke', and contains two hundred and nineteen names of people who owed sums ranging between 4d. and £3. The total value of debts due was £134 12s. 4d. His stock of yarn was worth just over £127. The branch of his business in which most of his profits were made was that of buying and selling linen cloth. In his house there was canvas cloth valued at £31 15s. 2d., and over £200 worth had been sent to London. The debts owing to him for cloth were enormous, and resulted in his goods and money amounting to the value of £2,344.

The appearance on the industrial scene of men such as Nugent, with large resources of capital, marks a distinct step forward in industrial organisation. A change was coming over the face of the Lancashire linen industry; the transition from an industry consisting of small but completely independent weavers and spinners, to one in which they were completely dependent for yarn and marketing of cloth, on the capitalist draper or clothier, had begun. Yet in Nugent's case the weavers were still buying raw materials which became their own property; Nugent was not simply handing out yarn to be woven and returned to him. There can be no doubt that at the end of the period covered by this study, as was the case with woollen manufacture, the transition was still only just getting under way.

[1] J. Aston, *Manchester Guide*, p. 29. Also in *Shuttleworth Accounts*, ii, p. 381.

E

CHAPTER V

TRADE AND MARKETS

SOME of the Lancashire cloth, both woollen and linen, was used locally. Every town must have had one or more small-scale draper or haberdasher who bought cloth from the manufacturer, with the simple aim of retailing it to other local people. A typical draper would have a shop in the town and might also tour the district selling and delivering cloth to customers.

William Awen was a draper who kept a shop in Manchester until his death in 1590. He bought rolls of cottons, friezes and kerseys, and sold them in his shop in gown or coat lengths. He was concerned only with local sales, and took no part in supplying raw materials, or in the weaving and finishing of cloth. At his death he had cloth in stock valued at over £20, and he concentrated on northern woollen cloth, leaving silks and other exotic cloths to the care of more enterprising drapers who had more capital. On his shelves were forty-five yards of white cottons worth 23s., and twenty yards of yellow and black cottons worth 9s. Thirty yards of grey frieze were valued at 28s. and he had small amounts of white and black frieze. The most expensive cloth in the shop was a hundred and eleven yards of various colours of kersey—blue, green, black, grey, white and plain—which averaged between 1s. 3d. and 1s. 6d. a yard.

Judging by the long list of debts due to Awen, it seems that much of his trade, no matter how minute the amount of cloth involved, was conducted on a credit basis, in the same way as the more ambitious business of wealthier clothiers who sold cloth outside Lancashire. Almost £18 was still due to be paid to Awen, at his death, by about fifty people, such as Edward Wright, who owed 2s. for four yards of white cottons, and John Taylor, 5s. for four yards of 'tawny fryce'. Mabel, the wife of Henry Prestwich, owed 25s. for 'several pieces of stuff'. On his travels around the district Awen had delivered three and a quarter yards of 'plain red', costing 2s. a yard and four yards of white cottons at 7d. a yard to a man named Edmund Birch on December 18th, 1589. The money was still unpaid when Awen died some six months later. In fact he had debtors in Salford, Rusholme, Chorlton, Stretford and a number of other hamlets and townships in the district.

Another local cloth retailer was Thomas Hardman who died in 1583, and used to call himself a mercer. He owned two shops, one at Manchester and one at Warrington where he kept all sorts of haberdashery, hardware and stationery, intended for local sale, although he did send some cloth to be sold in London.

Edward Holt of Wigan,[1] a successful linen draper, sold large quantities of linen cloth to local men, some to quite well-to-do gentlemen who must have used it for household requirements. Alexander Rigbie of Wigan, gentleman, owed Holt £10. Ralph Standanought, a linen draper of Dalton, near Wigan, who died in 1581, had sold linen cloth in smaller quantities to local men, including a parcel of cloth to a Warrington man who still owed him £3 12s. 3d.

One of the best examples of Lancashire cloth being used locally is provided by the activities of Dean Alexander Nowell who was in Lancashire as an executor of his brother's will. His brother was Robert Nowell, a lawyer, of Reade Hall, who had died in his London chambers in February, 1568. He stated in his will that he wanted some of his money to be spent to help the poor, so his brother Alexander, during the space of one week—July 3rd to July 10th, 1569—bought large quantities of woollen and linen cloth from over thirty Lancashire weavers and clothiers.[2] The cloth was to be distributed among the poor people of Burnley and Whalley parishes. It consisted of 2450 yards of woollens and 1800 yards of linen, for which Nowell paid a total of £327 4s. 9½d. This must have been quite a windfall for the weavers concerned. The man who sold the most cloth was Christopher Hindley who supplied Nowell with 732¼ yards of woollen cloth for which he paid out £45 16s. 10d. Another successful clothier was Richard Halstead of Burnley. He sold 651 yards of woollens, some of them rather more expensive than Hindley's cloth; the total cost was £46 2s. 2d. Richard Ingham of Cliviger, near Burnley, supplied 516¾ yards and received £36 18s. 2d. Three other men were each able to supply Nowell with cloth worth over £25. These were William Wigan of Blackburn, Nicholas Lache and Edward Birtwisle. These six men must have been among the most prosperous clothiers in the district, and so Nowell, probably wishing to help the weavers themselves as well as the poor people, also patronised a number of less wealthy weavers, who supplied him with more modest quantities. For instance, he bought 494 yards of linen cloth from Richard Howarth of Accrington, for £11 3s. 7d., some at 4d. a yard and some at 5d. Nicholas Sagar of Burnley sold him linens worth £2 7s. 9d., while James Whitehead, who had been elected constable of Habergham Eaves in 1567,[3] supplied him with 36 yards of linen costing 16s. 2d. Nowell also bought small batches of woollen cloth. William

[1] See *supra*, ch. iv, pp. 51–2.

[2] A. B. Grosart, *Towneley Hall MSS; The Spending of the Money of Robert Nowell*, p. 278 passim.   [3] Grosart, op. cit., p. 27.

Duxbury of Great Harwood sold him 44 yards of woollens at 1s. or 1s. 6d. a yard, at a total of £2 5s. 10d. One of the smallest sales was that of 26 yards of woollens at 1s. 4d. a yard by John Smith, who allowed Nowell to have the cloth for £1 14s. 4d., a deduction of 4d., perhaps for prompt payment.

The fact that Nowell was able to buy such large quantities of cloth in the short space of one week is ample evidence of the importance of the local cloth industries in the Burnley and Blackburn areas. There was enough cloth for Nowell to distribute worthwhile amounts for the making of various articles of clothing, to over seven hundred poor families in the parishes of Burnley and Whalley.

Large quantities of Lancashire cloth were taken out of the county and sold in towns all over England. Unfortunately it is impossible, as is the case with all sixteenth-century internal trade, whatever the commodity involved, to get any idea of the yearly averages or totals of cloth passing out of Lancashire, or how regular the flow of trade was between Lancashire and a particular town. The evidence allows only occasional glimpses of the trade taking place, so that the most that can be said is that a trade connection existed between Lancashire and a certain town.

Bearing in mind this reservation, one can say that there is evidence of Lancashire linen cloth being sold in Coventry, Banbury, Witney, Cambridge, Bedford, Newbury, Wellingborough, Northampton, Bury St. Edmunds, Daventry, Denbigh and Ruthin.[1] For instance, just before his death in 1597, Edward Holt, the Wigan linen draper, had cloth worth over £10 sold in Wellingborough, and men in Bedford, Cambridge and Bury St. Edmunds were in his debt for over £28. The other Wigan linen draper already mentioned was Ralph Standanought who supplied linen to Coventry and Northampton. When he died, two Coventry mercers still owed him £5 13s., and a Northampton man £1.

There seems to have been a regular connection between linen drapers of the Ormskirk area and the town of Denbigh. Two of the men who supplied linen to Denbigh were Thomas Smolte who in 1576 was owed £7 6s. by a Denbigh man, for linen cloth, and John Withington of Burscough, whose will of 1594 mentions three Denbigh men who owed him a total of £11 6s. for linens. A Liverpool linen draper, Robert Wolfall, who died in 1578, supplied small quantities of cloth to mercers in Denbigh and Ruthin. Robert Parr of Ruthin owed him £1 19s., while a Mr. Ashton of Denbigh owed £1.

Some linen merchants made the journey to distant towns in person to supervise the sale of their cloth. The names of several well travelled ones have survived. William Banester of Croston near Ormskirk, called himself a linen man in his will of 1595, and seems to have conducted a flourishing trade in linen cloth in the towns of Coventry, Banbury and Witney. On

---

[1] Wills and inventories of a number of linen drapers, quoted below.

the last trip before his death he had sold cloth worth over £138. Even so, it appears that he was unable to sell all the cloth he had taken with him. He left two packs with a man called Jackson in Banbury, at whose house he had stayed for a time, and he left another pack with a Mr. Waldeyne in Coventry, who had also acted as his host for a time. Apparently, both men had agreed to find buyers for Banester's unsold cloth.

Another linen draper, John Worthington of Warrington, made the long journey to Newbury in Berkshire shortly before his death in 1598, and stayed with Mr. Hancock, a barber, who lived 'behind the bridge in Newbury'. Worthington sold linen worth almost £28 to various drapers in the town, and although he called himself a linen draper in his will, that did not prevent him from dealing in woollen cloth too. During his stay in Newbury he managed to dispose of several pieces of grey frieze worth £10 7s. The whole of Worthington's trade, like that of all the other linen drapers, was carried out on a credit basis, with a date having been agreed upon when the money was to be paid to him.

Lancashire woollens also travelled widely, some going even further than the linens. They are known to have been sold in Halifax, Hull, Beverley,[1] Leicester, Stourbridge, Chester, Northampton, Norwich, Spalding, Loughborough, Hereford, London, Bristol and Southampton.

One of the earliest recorded sales of Lancashire woollen cloth in the sixteenth century took place about 1535, when John Webster, a Manchester 'clothman', as he called himself, supplied woollens worth £4 to Robert Forster, the Prior of Lawnaford in Herefordshire. At almost the same time Webster had sold £24 worth of cloth to Charles Eton, a Chester merchant.[2]

Some of the coarse woollens manufactured in the north-east of Lancashire around Burnley and Colne, were taken to Halifax, and from there probably followed the same paths as West Riding cloth. In the early 1540's for example, a Colne clothier, Christopher Mitchell, sold cloth valued at £31 to John Banester of Halifax.[3]

One of the main destinations of Lancashire woollens was London. There are a number of references to Lancashire men selling cloth there throughout the sixteenth century. One of the earliest instances surviving in the records was in 1543 when Edmund Sorocould of Manchester sold three packs of cottons for £20 to a citizen and haberdasher of London.[4] Twenty years later at least sixteen Lancashire clothiers visited Blackwell Hall to sell their cottons.[5] By this date there was a substantial trade in Lancashire cloth, so much so that there was a separate hall set aside for it along with the departments for other counties.[6]

---

[1] *Beverley Borough Records*, ed. J. Dennett, p. 57. For the rest, see below.
[2] C.1/1091/10.   [3] C.1/1034/41–5.   [4] C.1/1064/36.
[5] G. D. Ramsay, 'Distribution of the Cloth Industry in 1561–2', *E.H.R.*, LVII, 1942, pp. 361–9.   [6] A. Friis, *Alderman Cockayne's Project*, p. 27.

As might be expected, Lancashire clothiers went about the job of marketing the cloth in several different ways. Some made the journey personally and supervised the sale of their cloth. Richard Thornton of Ashton-under-Lyne travelled to London in 1553, where he sold ten packs of friezes. On the way southwards he made two calls, the first at Loughborough where he sold six packs of friezes, and then at Stourbridge Fair where he found a buyer for another six packs.[1] Twenty-two packs of friezes are quite a load for one man to deal with, so it is not surprising that Thornton took with him some sort of assistant, by the name of Robert Naden.

The sixteen Lancashire clothiers who traded at Blackwell Hall in 1561/2 had all made the journey in person. Five of them, George Holland, Edward Byddlestone, Humphrey Houghton, John Davie and Adam Hill, had travelled from Manchester, taking what the list calls 'kennett cottons'. Three others, Edward Cheetham, John Haworth and Giles Ainsworth were Bolton men, while John Hendell came from Blackburn.[2] For the other seven clothiers, the Blackwell Hall clerks have omitted to enter the home town. The market was open for the sale of cloth every Thursday noon until the following Saturday morning, so that these clothiers, who can have averaged no more than twenty miles a day, must have had to set out early on the Tuesday or Wednesday morning, nine or ten days before the opening of the sale they wished to attend. An even earlier start would be required if they intended to do business at Stourbridge Fair or at some other town on the journey southwards, so that a trip of this nature might mean as long as three or four weeks away from home. Often clothiers travelled together in a sort of caravan; there is a case in the Duchy Court[3] which shows seven Manchester clothiers travelling in this way to Stourbridge Fair in 1567. One of them was John Houghton whose load consisted of six packs of rugs.

A detailed account has survived of a trip made by Richard Nugent of Salford, which gives some idea of the intricacies and expenses involved in a long business journey.[4] Nugent was the son-in-law of George and Elizabeth Goldsmith of Manchester, who manufactured rugs and friezes. Later he became a wealthy linen draper,[5] but at the time of this trip in 1588, he was acting on behalf of his parents-in-law, and at the same time he had some connection with John Tipping, a Manchester linen draper.[6] He went to London and on the way home he called at Stourbridge. His receipts at London totalled £198 13s. 11d., and his expenses included

[1] *Pleadings in Duchy Court of Lancaster*, iii, p. 169.
[2] Ramsay, op. cit., pp. 361–9.   [3] D.L.1/87, L.1.
[4] Aston, op. cit., p. 29; and *Shuttleworth Accounts*, ii, p. 381.
[5] *supra*, ch. iv, p. 55.
[6] Perhaps a relative of the three Tipping brothers who were linen drapers in Manchester, see *supra*, ch. iv, p. 54.

13s. 5d. spent 'riding to London', £1 5s. 2d. 'for my own dyett in London', and 10s. 'for the standynge in the Fayre'. At Stourbridge he sold cloth worth £146 7s., and had to pay 13s. 4d. for the 'standynge in the Fayre', as well as similar expenses to those in London. The Stourbridge account also includes three personal items: 4d. 'for washing', 2d. 'for greasinge my bootes', and finally 3d., 'gav 'em in the house'.

The longest and most astonishing trips made in the sixteenth century by men from the north, were those to Southampton, which despite its great distance from the north of England, was frequently visited by merchants of Lancashire, and more regularly by merchants from even further afield, from Kendal. As early as February 21st, 1534/5, a 'Mr. Browtun' of Manchester brought ten horse-loads of cloth into Southampton.[1] According to the Southampton Cloth Hall Accounts, several Lancashire men were frequent visitors between 1569 and 1583. There were, for instance, Thomas Hardman of Bolton, and three Blackburn men, John Oldham, George Crompton and Nicholas Howarth. Some of the Kendal merchants used to call at Manchester on their way southwards and collect cloth which they took with them to Southampton. In 1581 and 1582, three of them, on more than one occasion, brought Manchester cottons to the cloth hall, along with their other cottons and kerseys. The double journey—Kendal to Southampton and back—took over four weeks, and even winter conditions did not prevent these northerners from travelling southwards just as frequently as in summer.[2]

Some clothiers, anxious perhaps to avoid the trouble, loss of time and expense involved in a long journey of this sort, did not make the trip themselves, but entrusted their cloth to a carrier or pack-horse-man. Richard Crompton of Bury had frequent dealings with a merchant in Chester. In 1547 he bought two packs of cottons at Manchester and sent them to Chester by carrier, even though the distance was comparatively short and the amount of cloth involved small.[3] William Madder of Radcliffe entrusted a pack of cottons to a man named James Hardier, in 1562.[4] The latter was instructed to carry the cottons to London and find a buyer for them. He was to have 3s. 4d. if he carried out the operation successfully.

Very often, however, clothiers did not permit a carrier to see to the marketing of the cloth. A carrier was usually expected to deliver the cloth to some other merchant who had agreed beforehand either to buy the cloth himself or to find someone else who wished to buy it. When Lawrence Robinson, the Salford clothier, died in 1587, he had recorded in his will that he had two packs of Rochdale friezes in London, one in the hands of

[1] B. C. Jones, 'Westmorland Packhorsemen in Southampton'; *Transactions of the Cumberland and Westmorland Antiquarian and Archæological Society*, LIX, 1960, pp. 65–84.
[2] ibid., p. 68.
[3] *Pleadings in Duchy Court of Lancaster*, iii, p. 8.   [4] D.L.1/46, M.5.

a Mr. Bullman, and the other at Blackwell Hall, as well as one pack of broad whites which had been delivered to a Mr. King. Both were citizens and haberdashers of London and had probably undertaken to find buyers for Robinson's cloth.

A flourishing family business might be fortunate enough to have a member of the family permanently in London to act as the receiver for cloth sent up from Lancashire. James Rillston, a Manchester cottonman, seems to have conducted a prosperous business in sending cottons to the London market. His cousin, George Hunt, had settled in London and become a citizen and haberdasher, and although Hunt was not exactly in partnership with his cousin, they did have some agreement by which Hunt received and bought some of Rillston's cloth. In 1578 Hunt owed his cousin £34 13s. for three packs of cottons; but he did not buy all Rillston's cloth: the will also mentions another citizen and haberdasher of London, Robert Hitchmonger, who was in debt for cottons—five packs valued at £52 15s.

There is a case in the Duchy Court of Lancaster which shows in some detail what may have been a common practice.[1] Two Rochdale men, Edmund Heyward and Arthur Heyley formed a partnership in 1566 with the aim of buying cloth and sending it to London. The initiative was taken by Heyward, but since he lacked capital, he had to rely on Heyley, whose good name would provide surety to the weavers whose cloth they bought. They agreed to share the profits equally, and bought eight pieces of cottons from Heyward's brother James, and a further six pieces from a Ralph Smith. The cottons were done up into two packs and entrusted to John Feather, a carrier, who was instructed to deliver them to Roger Heyley,[2] 'dwellinge in London'. Along with the cottons they sent a letter authorising Roger Heyley to sell the cottons to 'what persons he should thinke good, and further, to take suche dayes of paimente with them as to his own discretion'. The carrier was given 11s. 4d. for his pains before he set out from Rochdale. He delivered the cottons safely to Roger Heyley who proceeded to sell them for £20 to a London merchant.

These transactions provide some clue as to the amount of profit which the Rochdale men could expect to make when dealing in cloth in quantities of this size. They bought the cottons originally for £17 6s., which with the carrier's fee made a total expenditure of £17 17s. 4d. Of the £20 owing to them therefore, £2 2s. 8d. would be clear profit.

This particular case also shows most effectively that the dealings which many country clothiers had with merchants who bought their cloth, were often far from straightforward. The credit system was bristling with difficulties and dangers. In the transactions so far no money had exchanged hands. James Heyward and Ralph Smith, the weavers, received no pay-

[1] D.L.1/72, H.25.
[2] There is no mention of whether or not Roger Heyley was a relative of Arthur.

ment from the two partners. Instead, Arthur Heyley signed a bond with them, promising to pay them as soon as the cloth was sold in London, and he had received the cash from that sale. But the partners would receive no payment until Roger Heyley had succeeded in finding a buyer, which might take a considerable period, for all they knew. Even then payment might not be immediate, because that buyer too would probably require credit. In actual fact the buyer was John Clothier, citizen and merchant of London, who agreed to pay the £20 to Roger Heyley, within two months. Thus if things ran smoothly, the four Rochdale men could expect at least a two months' wait for payment and profit.

Unfortunately for the northern men, business did not run smoothly on this occasion. There were frequent trade depressions during the sixteenth century, which, though short, still played havoc with the sale and export of cloth. It may have been one of these depressions which caused John Clothier to become suddenly bankrupt, before two months elapsed. On the other hand, it may have had nothing to do with a trade depression: a merchant can of course become bankrupt without there being a trade depression, but whatever the reason, the fact remains that Clothier did become bankrupt, and as far as the partners were concerned there was no hope either of recovering the cottons themselves or the money owing for them. At this point, Edward Heyward, the originator of the scheme, realising that he was about to lose quite seriously, denied that he had ever made an agreement with Arthur Heyley. Not to be outdone, the latter, attempting to force Heyward to bear his share of the losses, brought a case against his partner in the Duchy Court, in which he bewailed the fact that he himself was a very poor man. Unfortunately the outcome of the case, as with so many of the Duchy Court cases, is obscure, but whatever happened someone was bound to lose heavily. It was likely to be Arthur Heyley since he himself admitted that his agreement with Heyward had never been put in writing, and that the weavers of the cloth still held the bonds that he had signed. The only person who gained any profit at all from this ill-fated venture was the carrier who received his payment before he left for London.

This was not the only type of mishap that could befall a country clothier. A case in Chancery[1] provides an instance of a clothier claiming that he had lost bonds given to him by the customer, and then having to resort to a lawsuit to recover the debt. James Webster, a Manchester 'clothman', sold £24 worth of cloth to a Chester merchant, and £4 worth to the prior of Lawnaford Abbey in Herefordshire, somewhere about 1535. He took bonds which proved the transactions and fixed a date at which payment was to be made. Four years later Webster brought a suit against both men in Chancery. He claimed that he had lost the bonds, and that knowing this, his debtors refused to pay. In a case of this sort one is never

[1] C.1/1091/10.

quite sure which was the guilty party, because the verdicts are usually obscure. This case was no exception, but it does show how the credit system was open to all kinds of abuse, and provided both clothier and customer with opportunities for sharp practice, if they felt so inclined.

Another Lancashire man who was involved in a lawsuit,[1] was Edmund Sorocould, the Salford clothier. In 1543 he sold three packs of cottons for £20 to Anthony Payne, citizen and haberdasher of London. The money was to be paid at the Feast of St. Bartholomew. But in the meantime Payne 'mindynge to defraud (your) poor orator and others his creditors of their juste debtes . . . departed out of the realme or otherwise fled or prively absented himself', though not before he had appointed another London haberdasher, Richard King, as his deputy. All Payne's goods were to be in the 'survey and governmente' of King, who 'might retaine them as his owne goodes'. The latter, by no means a slow worker, immediately seized eight packs of cloth belonging to Payne, which were lying in a warehouse at Southampton waiting to be shipped abroad, removed Payne's seal from the packs, and substituted his own, to prevent Edmund Sorocould and other debtors claiming any of the packs to satisfy Payne's debts. It emerged later that King was holding the Salford man's cloth in a cellar in London, claiming that it was to satisfy his own debts owing to him by Payne, 'which he falsely surmised to be due'. In the end, but only after a great deal of delay, King was ordered to pay Sorocould the £20.

To round off this chapter of accidents, it may be pointed out that another unfortunate fate that could befall a clothier was a complete failure to sell cloth which he had taken. The Goldsmiths seem to have suffered a setback of this sort about the time of Elizabeth Goldsmith's death in 1588. Her inventory contains the item 'Clothe lyinge at London in Blakewell Hall, yt was lefte unsould atte London Fayre, Ao dni. 1588'.[2] The goods were four packs of friezes valued at £35 9s.

When it arrived in London, Lancashire cloth passed into the hands of the merchant who would be responsible for its export to the continent of Europe. Apparently Manchester cottons were mostly exported to France in the middle years of the century. In 1560 a report from the Merchant Adventurers to the Privy Council stated that 'Bristow frizes, Welsh cottons, and the most part of Manchester cottons are spent and consumed in France; the rest in Italy and Spain, and some in the Low Countries'.[3]

There is also among the Domestic State Papers, a later document[4] written between 1575 and 1585, probably by a West Country merchant, which professes to be 'a speciall direction for divers trades of merchaundize',

---

[1] C.1/1064/36.   [2] Aston, op. cit., p. 28.
[3] S.P.D., Eliz., 15, no. 67. Quoted by Mendenhall, op. cit., p. 57.
[4] Tawney and Power, op. cit., iii, pp. 199–210.

and which states that Manchester cottons were to be sent to all parts of Galicia,[1] to Bordeaux in Gascony,[2] and to Bayonne and Portugal.[3]

The Port Books show that this was indeed the case, and they certainly bear out the Merchant Adventurers' report, revealing that the bulk of Lancashire cloth exported from London in the sixteenth century was shipped to France. Another point revealed by the Port Books is that Rouen took the majority of Lancashire cloth entering France. Again this is not a surprising discovery, since Robert Hitchcock wrote in his 'Pollitique Platt' for the development of fisheries, in 1580, that 'at Rone in Fraunce which is the chefest vent, be solde our Englishe wares, as Welche and Manchester Cottons'.[4]

It was London which handled the major proportion of outgoing Lancashire textiles; the London Port Books make this abundantly clear, and, together with one or two other documents, supply much information about trade after 1565, though not nearly so much as might have been hoped. For the sixteenth century, only three books have survived which throw any light on the export of Lancashire cloth; the first two each deal only with half a year, Easter to Michaelmas, 1565,[5] and the same period in 1576.[6] It is not until the end of the century that there is a book covering a whole year, and that is the year beginning Michaelmas 1598.[7] Moreover, especially in the first and last of these three books there is often no distinction drawn between the various types of cottons exported, whether they were Manchester, northern, Welsh, Kendal, or Cheshire cottons. This means that very few of the figures quoted can be strictly accurate, and those for trade at the end of the century can only be regarded as minimum figures. Yet in spite of all the information which the Port Books do not tell, it is still possible to get some invaluable glimpses into an otherwise completely obscure branch of the textile trade.

In the first place, it is immediately obvious that the main type of Lancashire cloth being exported through London was cottons, with only rare mention of other types of Lancashire woollens and none at all of linen cloth. The 1565 Port Book[8] does little more than lend proof to what might already have been suspected: that Manchester cottons were being exported at that date. Eight Manchester cottons were shipped to Vigo on August 1st. Their coarseness is indicated by the fact that they were being used as wrappers for some of the other cloth cargo, the more sophisticated Suffolk and Gloucester short cloths. There are other entries of cottons for that half year, but not one of them is specified. They may have been Manchester cottons, but equally well they could have been any of the four other types of cottons.

---

[1] ibid., p. 200.   [2] ibid., p. 205.   [3] ibid., p. 203.
[4] R. Hitchcock, 'Pollitique Platt'; quoted by Tawney and Power, op. cit., iii, p. 254.
[5] E190, 2/1.   [6] E190, 6/4.   [7] E190, 10/11.
[8] E190, 2/1.

The two remaining Port Books are much more helpful in throwing light on the activities of the London export merchants. The great pity is that only these two isolated periods can be studied, so that it is impossible, at least from the Port Books, to get any idea of the fluctuations in trade, or to see how Lancashire cloth fared during periods of depression. The first of the two books[1] shows that in the eleven years since Port Books were introduced, an amazing change had come over the trade in Lancashire textiles. In the half year beginning at Easter 1576, a total of 67,154 goads of Manchester cottons was exported from London to the continent of Europe. This figure forms about 43% of the total of 156,161 goads of cottons of all kinds exported during that half year. The amount of Manchesters exported was not much smaller than that of their great rival, Welsh cottons, of which 79,537 goads were exported. The remainder consisted of 3,020 goads of 'northern cottons', which may have been manufactured in Lancashire, and 2,600 goads of Chester or Cheshire cottons.[2] There also took place during that period a solitary shipment of friezes that can definitely be identified as Lancashire friezes—five pieces to Emden on September 14th.

Of the 67,154 goads of Manchester cottons exported through London, 52,956 were sent to France, and of these, 36,450 goads were bound for Rouen. Dunkirk was a poor second, taking 6,400 goads. Bordeaux took 3,422, La Rochelle 2,848, and Bayonne 2,146 goads. There was a single shipment of 1,000 goads to Le Havre, one of 650 goads to Dieppe and a very small one of 40 goads to Calais.[3] It is interesting to note that Manchester cottons exports showed more diversity than their Welsh rivals, of which 95% of London exports went to Rouen in that half year. The second best customer for Lancashire cloth was Spain, which took 4,658 goads of Manchester cottons, the majority of which were described as being bound for Galicia. The remaining cottons were divided between Danzig, St. Nicholas in Russia, Hamburg, Antwerp and Flushing.[4]

Unfortunately we are not permitted another glimpse of the export figures until 1594/5, when a document in the Domestic State Papers throws some light on the problem.[5] It is most unfortunate that the Port Books and other documents leave a complete blank for the years between 1576 and 1594, because it prevents us from seeing how badly the trade in Lancashire cloth was affected during the troubled years after 1585. It is well known that military operations in the struggle between Spain and the rebellious Netherlands closed or partly closed the chief ports of entry for English cloth destined for the markets of Germany and central Europe. Sometimes the lines of communication from the ports to those areas were cut. In 1585 for instance, the Duke of Parma captured Brussels, Ghent

[1] E190, 6/4.
[2] See table 4. p. 69. The goad was 1½ yards.   [3] See table 5, p. 70.
[4] See table 5.   [5] S.P.D., Eliz., 253, no. 122.

and Antwerp, which was afterwards blockaded by the Sea Beggars, causing complete strangulation of its trade. When Nymwegen was taken by the Spaniards in 1585, it gave them control of the Rhine and cut communications between northern ports and Germany.[1] Nor was Emden very satisfactory at this time because it was uncomfortably close to Spanish held Groningen, and the Dutch themselves were blockading it in an attempt to cut off food supplies to the Spanish occupied territories. When England herself came into the war against Spain in 1585, she naturally lost the Spanish and Portuguese markets, and even the French markets were threatened when Philip II ordered the seizure of as many English ships as possible.

Thus by the end of 1586 the export trade in English cloth had become so slack that clothiers were complaining to the Privy Council[2] and a Spanish agent in England gleefully reported the results in November, 1586, with some exaggeration and some slight errors of fact:

They are much troubled with this war which they have entered into against Spain, as the whole country is without trade, and knows not how to recover it; the shipping and commerce here having mainly depended upon the communication with Spain and Portugal. They feel the deprivation all the more now with the loss of the cloth trade with Germany, which they formerly carried on through Holland and up the Rhine, but have now been deprived of. . . . The rest of their trade . . . is a mere trifle. . . . Their French trade is very insignificant, and is carried on by a few small vessels only.[3]

In fact, it may be that Lancashire cottons did not suffer quite so much as some other types of cloth, since France had been the main market for them before the war. The Spanish agent is not strictly accurate when he claims that the French trade was 'very insignificant'. Even so, it is not surprising to find that some Lancashire clothiers, especially those dealing in friezes which are known to have been sent to Emden before the war, were experiencing great difficulty in selling their cloth. One of them was John Robinson who in 1587 was unable to sell four packs of friezes at Stourbridge Fair. In the same year Lawrence Robinson of Salford had cloth worth over £30 which he could not sell as easily as usual. Some of it was at Blackwell Hall, and the rest was in the hands of two London merchants, Messrs. Bullman and King, who had not succeeded in finding a buyer. In 1588, Elizabeth Goldsmith had four packs of friezes left unsold at Blackwell Hall.[4]

This particular crisis was probably fairly short-lived, for at the end of 1587 an agreement was made for trading at Stade, Spanish troops were

---

[1] J. D. Gould, 'The Crisis in the Export Trade, 1586–1587', *E.H.R.*, LXXI, 1956, pp. 212–22.

[2] ibid., p. 213.

[3] *Calendar of State Papers, Spanish, 1580–1586*, No. 505, pp. 651–2.

[4] Aston, op. cit., p. 28.

withdrawn from Guelderland, and by the end of 1588, Middelburg had recovered its prosperity.[1] However, the Spanish markets were still out of bounds, and although the worst of the crisis might have been over, the markets were far from having recovered completely. According to the document in the State Papers,[2] in the year 1594/5 a total of 168,065 goads of cottons of all types were exported through London. The share of Manchester cottons was small—only 19,669 goads; but the amount of northern cottons had increased remarkably and stood at 53,942 goads. This description—northern cottons—presents us with the problem of trying to decide where they were produced. It is probably reasonable to assume that some of them at least were manufactured in Lancashire towns other than Manchester—Blackburn, Bolton or Bury for instance, where cottons are known to have been produced. Admittedly, however, cottons were also produced further northwards, and also in Cheshire, although often the Port Books take the trouble to mention that a particular batch of cloth was Chester cottons or Kendal cottons. The truth is, however, that exactly how many of these northern cottons had been made in Lancashire and how many elsewhere, will never be known. The best that can be done is to combine the totals of Manchester and northern cottons and say that in the year 1594/5, 73,611 goads of cottons made in the north of England were exported through London, not a particularly impressive figure when one remembers that 70,174 goads were exported in only half a year in 1576; even allowing for the fact that the 1576 half year was from Easter to Michaelmas—always the busier of the two for trade—1594/5 was clearly not the best of years. Whether it was better or worse than the preceding years, however, is impossible to say. Nor incidentally, did Welsh cottons fare much better: they totalled 87,365 goads, again not much more than the amount exported in the 1576 half year.[3]

Statistics for the year 1598/9 are provided by the London Port Book,[4] which presents the same problem as the State Paper, in that it too mentions large quantities of northern cottons. In that year only 13,288 goads are specifically labelled as Manchester cottons, while northern cottons numbered 59,180 goads, making a total of 72,468 goads of cottons which can definitely be identified as having been manufactured in the north of England. This appears to be a slight fall from the 1594/5 figure, but in actual fact this was not the case: the picture is complicated somewhat by a large number of entries in the Port Book labelled either 'welsh and northern cottons' or 'northern and welsh cottons', with no indication of the amounts of each. These add up to the significant total of 37,000 goads; exactly how many northern cottons were concealed within this figure, it is impossible to say, but there were certainly enough for one to draw the conclusion that 1598/9 was a much better year for cottons

[1] Gould, op. cit., p. 220.
[3] See table 4.

[2] S.P.D., Eliz., 253, no. 122.
[4] E190, 10/11.

exports as a whole than 1594/5, and was more comparable with the successful half year in 1576. In addition to the cottons already mentioned, there were 2,095 goads described as 'Manchester and Welsh' cottons, making the total cottons exports for the year, including Welsh cottons, 211,082 goads.[1]

As to the distribution of the cottons exports, the market was dominated by France, even more so than it had been in 1576. The vast majority of the north of England cottons were shipped to France, which took 67,480 goads out of the 72,468 goads exported from London. In France, Rouen was still by far the chief port of entry for Manchester and northern cottons, handling 49,560 goads during the year. The only other French port to handle northern cottons in any significant quantities was Dieppe, at which 16,650 goads of northern and Manchesters were imported.[2] Most of the other markets of 1576 had dropped out of the picture, and only St. Nicholas continued her imports of cottons. There were no new markets of any significance.

Table 4. Exports of cottons from London (in goads)

Type of cottons	1576 (half year)	1594/5	1598/9
Manchester	67,154	19,669	13,288
northern	3,020	53,942	59,180
Chester	2,600		
Welsh and Chester	2,000		
Manchester and Welsh	1,850		2,095
northern and Welsh		1,400	37,000
Welsh	79,537	87,365	99,519
unspecified		5,689	
	156,161	168,065	211,082

Northern cottons continued to be exported through London in the seventeenth century, and the level appears to have kept fairly stable. For some reason or other, however, their Welsh rivals began to fall far behind in the early years of the seventeenth century. In 1620 for instance, three times as many northern cottons as Welsh were shipped to Rouen in four months; while by 1641, 68,320 goads of northern cottons were shipped there. This was about 80% of all northern cottons exported through

---

[1] There is a slight discrepancy between these figures and those given by T. C. Mendenhall, op. cit., p. 54, who mentions Welsh cottons exports of 130,232 goads and 'other cottons' at 80,850 goads. To arrive at these figures he has apparently assumed that about 30,000 out of the 37,000 goads of Welsh and northern cottons were in fact, Welsh. However, the cottons which can definitely be identified as Welsh were slightly under 100,000 goads. This, of course, does not invalidate the general conclusion that 1598/9 was a good year for cottons exports as a whole.

[2] See table 5, p. 70.

Table 5. Destinations of Manchester and northern cottons exported from London (in goads)

	1576 (half year)			1598/9		
	Manchesters	northerns	total	Manchesters	northerns	total
Rouen	36,450	800	37,250	5,400	44,160	49,560
Dunkirk	6,400	none	6,400			none
Bordeaux	3,422	none	3,422			none
Bayonne	2,146	none	2,146			none
La Rochelle	2,848	200	3,048	120	1,150	1,270
Le Havre	1,000	none	1,000			none
Dieppe	650	300	950	5,300	11,350	16,650
Calais	40	none	40			none
Galicia (N. Spain)	3,300	none	3,300			none
St. Lucar	798	1,000	1,798			none
Biscay	440	700	1,140			none
Bilbao	120	none	120			none
Danzig	3,500	none	3,500			none
Hamburg	2,620	none	2,620			none
Antwerp	1,100	20	1,120			none
Flushing	200	none	200			none
St. Nicholas	2,120	none	2,120	2,410	320	2,730
Amsterdam			none	none	600	600
Leghorn			none	none	200	200
unspecified			none	58	1,400	1,458
	67,154	3,020	70,174	13,288	59,180	72,468

London that year, and over four times the amount of Welsh cottons entering Rouen in the same period.[1]

The men who shipped Lancashire cottons abroad are worthy of some investigation. All the evidence points to the fact that these merchants were, with only rare exceptions, members of one or other of the great London Livery Companies. There is not a single instance of Lancashire cloth being shipped by a man who had made the journey from Lancashire for that specific purpose, though occasionally one comes across Lancashire men who had settled in London years before, and become citizens and members of one of the companies: Nicholas Mosley and George Hunt were both Manchester men who had established themselves in the City. This was only to be expected, since the only people normally allowed to ship cloth from London were freeman of the City. In the well documented half year from Easter to Michaelmas 1576, almost sixty London merchants handled Lancashire cottons, although most of the cloth was concentrated in the hands of about a dozen of them. Appropriately enough, the chief exporter of Lancashire cloth was a Lancashire man, Nicholas Mosley, who had settled in London about 1568, as the London partner in the family business, based at Manchester.[2] He became a member of the Clothworkers' Company and was soon receiving and exporting large amounts of Lancashire cottons. In the half year in 1576 he was responsible for shipping 10,150 goads of Manchester cottons to Rouen, well over one quarter of all Manchester cottons sent to that port. He also shipped small quantities of Welsh cottons to Rouen. Nicholas Mosley did not always attend himself to the shipping of cloth. Very often one of his assistants, another northerner, Edward Sorocould, is mentioned in the Port Book as having acted on behalf of his master. On three occasions it was Rowland Mosley instead of his father, who saw to the shipping of cloth. In 1589 Nicholas became an Alderman of the City of London, and was still exporting Lancashire cloth in 1598, even though he must have been well over seventy by then. Later on he became Lord Mayor and was knighted, and died in 1612 at the age of 85. In the Mosley Family Memoirs[3] appears this epitaph to the illustrious Sir Nicholas, who made a fortune and became famous through trading in Lancashire cottons:

Here lyes the worthy wight which once was poore and bare,
Yet after prov'd a Knight by beinge London's Meare;
Here lyes that worthy clothiar whose cloth was dyde in grayne—
It bootes not who was the loser soe he therby did gayne.
Here lyes Sir Nicholas Moseley, as you should understande,
Heye Shereffe once of Lancaster, wheyrin be bought much lande,

---

[1] Mendenhall, op. cit., p. 61.
[2] R. Hollingworth, *Mancuniensis*, p. 101.
[3] *Mosley Family Memoirs*, 1849, quoted by Wadsworth and Mann, p. 9.

F

Fower hundred pound in gold he had within his bed they toke it from
A thousay pound a year perforce he left behjnde hym
Unto his sonne and heir. . . .
Here he was born, at London he was bredde,
Hence drewe he trade, which thence he uttered,
To Russe, to Tartasie, Fraunce, and Italy
Your home spunne cloth hee yearly made to see.

As far as the figures show, no other merchant exported anything like so many Manchester cottons as Nicholas Mosley. His nearest rival was George Stoddard, a citizen and grocer, who in 1576 accounted for 5,250 goads, all to Rouen, except for a single shipment of 1,000 goads to Le Havre. Thomas Starkie, who was a member of the Skinners' Company and who later became an alderman, shipped 4,300 goads of Manchester cottons to Rouen; in the same period he was also the chief exporter of Welsh cottons, being responsible for 10,500 goads, all to Rouen. In fact in the 1576 half year Starkie shipped more cottons of both sorts combined than any other merchant—14,800 goads in all.

In addition to these three men, there were seven others who each shipped more than 2,000 goads of Manchester cottons; men such as Thomas Danser, a girdler, Bernard Field, grocer, Thomas Pullison, an alderman, and Edward Barclay and Michael Locke, who were both described as mercers. Locke shipped all the cottons which went to Russia for the Russia Company, of which he was the London agent.[1] Two merchant tailors, John Farmer and William Gifford, shared the 3,300 goads which were sent to Galicia (N. Spain).

There were one or two exceptions to this pattern of Lancashire cottons being shipped by Londoners or by Lancastrians living in London. There was one foreign merchant, Werner Ellebeck, a Hanser, who exported 440 goads to Hamburg in a German ship. There was in addition, the unique case of two Ipswich men, John Napp and John Fisher, who sent 108 goads to St. Lucar.

In 1598/9, only thirty-five merchants are recorded as having dealt in Manchester or northern cottons. Most of the 1576 merchants had disappeared from the scene, though Nicholas Mosley was still active. He was no longer a leading exporter, however, and only handled 1,150 goads of Manchester cottons. By this time he had become a member of the Russia Company and so enjoyed certain trading privileges in Russia granted to members of the Company by the Tsar Boris in 1598. Apparently Nicholas was indulging in a bit of illicit trading, since he sent 450 goads of Manchester cottons privately to St. Nicholas, not as a member of the Russia Company.[2]

[1] T. S. Willan, *The Early History of the Russia Company, 1553–1603*, p. 26.
[2] T. S. Willan, 'Trade between England and Russia in the Second Half of the Sixteenth Century', *E.H.R.*, LXIII, 1948, pp. 307–21.

The leading exporter of Lancashire cloth in 1598 was John Woodward, a member of the Ironmongers' Company, who was responsible for transporting 8,500 goads of Manchester and northern cottons to France. He was closely followed by William Leveson, with 7,300 goads to France, and Augustine Skinner, another ironmonger, who shipped 5,300 goads of northern cottons to France. There were eight others who shipped over 2,000 goads each, including Reynold Green, a cutler, Edward Skaggs, Richard Symes, ironmonger, and two girdlers, Robert Bell and John Potter, working in partnership.

These merchants did not restrict themselves to dealing in one type of cottons, but could usually be found shipping Welsh cottons and other types of cloth as well. The two girdlers shipped 12,300 goads of Welsh cottons to France in 1598/9, and were the chief exporters of Welsh cottons in that year. Edward Skaggs stood high on the list of exporters of Welsh cottons, and also shipped quantities of single bays to Rouen. Richard Symes sent quantities of plain greys to Dieppe, as well as his 5,010 goads of cottons.

In this year, 1598/9, the cloth exported to Russia was again recorded in the name of the Russia Company's agent, except for the surreptitious activities of Sir Nicholas Mosley. This agent was Anthony Marler, who shipped 2,275 goads of cottons, mostly Manchesters, to St. Nicholas.

This concentration on London as the chief outlet for Lancashire woollens must not be allowed to obscure the fact that there were other ports which handled Lancashire cloth in significant quantities, though their share of the trade was naturally much smaller than London's. Three of these ports were Chester, Liverpool and Bristol. Although several Port Books have survived for each of these centres during the sixteenth century, they contain the same pitfalls as the London ones. It would have been interesting to assess the rôle of each port by comparing the quantities of Manchester cottons exported from each of the four in the same period. Unfortunately this is impossible: often two ports can be studied in the same year; the books for both Chester and Liverpool have survived for the year 1565/6, and for 1582/3. Bristol and Liverpool can be observed during 1573/4. But there is not a single year in the sixteenth century for which useful Port Books have survived for all four ports.

In spite of this it is still possible to get a vague idea of the comparative rôles of the lesser ports. It is immediately obvious, for instance, that Chester played a very respectable part in exporting Manchester cottons, and it had done so for many years before Port Books began to be kept regularly. In 1547 the corporation of Chester had ordered that 'all merchaunts of Manchester and ther abouts that bringe any cottons to this citie to be soulde shalle bringe the same to the said comen haule and pay for every ten peses of cottons id'.[1] In the year beginning Michaelmas

[1] R. H. Morris, *Chester under the Plantagenets and Tudors*, p. 399.

1565[1] Chester handled a total of 25,600 goads of Manchester cottons, a far from negligible amount. Unfortunately the figures for London at this time have not survived, the earliest full total being the 67,154 goads exported in the half year, Easter to Michaelmas, 1576. In actual fact the Chester total for the Easter to Michaelmas half year in 1566 was 11,400 goads of Manchester cottons. This sort of comparison with ten years between the two is obviously rather unreal, but it does show that in 1565/6 Chester had a significant share of the total Manchester cottons exported from England.

The Chester merchants were concerned to safeguard their trade against competition from other ports, and in 1580 they sent a petition to the Privy Council asking that Chester might be made the only port from which Manchester cottons could be exported.[2] Surprisingly this request was granted,[3] although the Privy Council must have realised that it was impossible to exclude London, Bristol and even Liverpool from the export trade in cottons; they all continued and ignored Chester's claims. In 1582, Chester's exports of Manchester cottons, instead of increasing, were somewhat lower than the 1565 figures.[4] They amounted to 17,550 goads in the year beginning Michaelmas 1582. After that the scene remains obscure until exactly ten years later, when the Port Book[5] shows that the legitimate trade in Manchester cottons had ceased almost entirely, having been heavily dependent on the Spanish markets. There was only a single shipment of 110 goads to France. Chester's dependence on this Spanish trade had been especially apparent in 1566 when about 75% of the cottons exported found their way to that country, the rest being divided between Bordeaux and La Rochelle.[6] In 1582/3 the situation was similar, Spain taking 13,950 goads and France 3,600. Shortly after this, both markets must have been destroyed by the war.

We have no further knowledge of Chester's trade until 1600.[7] In the first six months of that year there were again no shipments of Manchester cottons to the continent, but there were two very small quantities sent to Ireland. One consisted of nine 'ends' of Manchester cottons, containing 89 yards, and the other was four pieces of cottons valued at 48s. And that was all.

The merchants who indulged in the trade at Chester were numerous. In 1565/6 twenty-seven merchants exported Manchester cottons. Only two men handled more than 2,000 goads, however; one of them, John Middleton of Chester, was responsible for the shipping of 3,200 goads. He was assisted by another Chester merchant, William Massey, who acted as a factor for Middleton on one occasion, when he shipped 200 goads of

[1] E190, 1323/1 and 1323/10.   [2] S.P.D. Add. vol. xxvi, p. 90.
[3] S.P.D. clviii., 2; both quoted by Daniels, op. cit., p. 7; and by Hewart, op. cit., p. 25.
[4] E190, 1325/8.   [5] E190, 1328/5.
[6] Spain took 19,900 goads; France 5,700 goads.   [7] E190, 1327/28.

Manchester cottons aboard the *Nicholas*, bound for Biscay in Spain. Massey was a merchant on his own account as well, and he exported 950 goads to Vigo. William Hewett was the other leading cottons exporter, and besides shipping 2,450 goads of cottons, seems to have dealt on occasions with coal. On June 11th, 1566, he sent fifty tons of coal to La Rochelle. Apart from these two men, however, the other Chester merchants handled cottons only on a very small scale. Most of them made no more than three shipments during the whole year, and thirteen of them sent only one consignment, of usually somewhere in the region of 300 goads. The same was true of the year 1582/3 when, of the twenty-two merchants who exported Manchester cottons, thirteen made only one shipment, and only one man, Roger Hanmer, managed to pass the 2,000 goads mark. Five men had well over a thousand goads to their name, which helps to explain why the total export was so high.

The export trade was not entirely in the hands of native Chester merchants. A Liverpool man and a merchant from Newcastle[1] each shipped a few hundred goads of cottons through Chester in 1566. Edward Mosley travelled from Blackburn and visited the custom house at Chester on July 13th of that year, bringing with him 450 goads of Manchester cottons and ten pieces of 'Yorkshire straights'. They were shipped aboard a foreign vessel, the *Nostra Seignora* of Portugal which was to take them to 'Portigalett in Spain'. Out of a total of eighteen vessels which carried Manchester cottons from Chester in 1566, only two were foreign. The other was the *Santa Maria de Tolaio* from Varmut, in Spain.

Five useful Port Books have survived for Liverpool which enable one to examine what part the Lancashire port played in the export of the county's textiles. These books reveal that throughout the second half of the sixteenth century, until the disturbances and the war with Spain put a stop to it, there was a steady if rather modest stream of Lancashire cottons finding their way to the continent of Europe through Liverpool. The earliest surviving record of this trade is one provided by the Liverpool Town Books which mention that in 1558 two French ships were in the port, and they had brought wines which the French exchanged for cottons.[2]

In the year beginning Michaelmas 1565 Liverpool was the point of departure for 6,900 goads of Manchester cottons: 4,700 went to Bilbao and the remainder to Lisbon.[3] This is obviously a very modest amount, when compared with the trade of another outport—Chester—whose figure for the same year was 25,600 goads.

Six years later the Liverpool exports had increased somewhat, and had

---

[1] Which Newcastle it was is not stated, though one would expect it to have been Newcastle-under-Lyme.

[2] *Liverpool Town Books*, I, p. 127.

[3] Two books: E190, 1323/4 and 1323/9.

reached the total of 8,700 goads.[1] That year saw a marked redistribution of the trade; whereas six years earlier no cottons had been sent to France now 7,000 goads of Manchesters were shipped to St. Jean de Luz, leaving no more than 1,700 to Bilbao. Perhaps this year was not typical, however, since the next two glimpses of Liverpool exports show the balance restored in favour of Spain, almost to the exclusion of France.

The year 1575/6 saw 5,600 goads shipped from Liverpool, all to Bilbao, except for a solitary shipment of 800 goads to La Rochelle.[2] The final glimpse permitted by the Port Books before the war with Spain put an end to the Spanish trade, was in 1582/3[3] when 7,000 goads of Manchester cottons were despatched overseas, again all to Bilbao, except for one shipment of 600 goads, which deserves special notice, because it was the first recorded shipment of Manchester cottons on such a scale to Ireland. Ever since 1565 Ireland had taken steady supplies of Kendal cottons and Yorkshire cloth, but never before such a significant quantity of Manchester cottons.

In the good years before the war the activities of the exporting merchants at Liverpool were very similar to those of their Chester counterparts. Every year there were between ten and fifteen men who exported cottons, but most of them sent only one shipment, sometimes of no more than a hundred goads. But there was one unusual feature about the Liverpool trade, not to be seen quite so markedly at the other ports. This was the presence of more than just an occasional merchant who was not a native of Liverpool. Chester merchants often sent shipments of cottons through Liverpool. These 'foreign' merchants were especially noticeable in 1572/3 when seven of the sixteen merchants involved in the cottons trade were not Liverpool men. Peter Newall of Chester, for instance, was in Liverpool on January 9th, 1572/3, when he exported 400 goads of Manchester cottons. On the same day he acted as agent or factor for three other Chester merchants who between them were intending to export a further one thousand goads.

Two merchants from the continent also appeared in Liverpool during that year. Peter du Pirrie came from Bordeaux and bought three hundred goads of Manchester cottons, which he shipped to Spain, along with some copper and 1,500 'broke fells', in the *Henry Bonaventure* of Liverpool. On July 20th, 1573 there was a Spanish vessel at Liverpool, the *Marrye* of St. Vincent. On board was 'Marten de Vyrrye of Sububurra in Fraunce', who bought ten packs of Manchester cottons containing 3,400 goads, and had them shipped to St. Jean de Luz. This is a surprisingly large quantity for a single merchant to ship all at one time; in fact it is the largest recorded

[1] E190, 1324/4.
[2] E190, 1324/9. On October 12th, 1575, one piece of Manchester kersey was shipped to Drogheda by an Irish merchant.
[3] E190, 1325/1.

single consignment of Manchester cottons made by one merchant from any port in the whole of the sixteenth century.

The fact that the usual run of merchants trading at Liverpool sent only a few hundred goads at a time, usually meant that a group of them would fill up one vessel with their consignments, and in the better years as many as six vessels would leave for the continent, sometimes singly, sometimes in twos, but never more than two at a time, carrying nothing but cottons. One of the first sailings from Liverpool to the continent recorded in a Port Book, was that made by the *Henry* of Liverpool to Bilbao in April 1566.[1] The cargo consisted of 1,700 goads of Manchester cottons, whose ownership was shared by five Liverpool merchants and one from Chester.

Merchants shipping cloth abroad sometimes met difficulties and inconveniences just as the country clothiers did. On July 20th, 1573, six Liverpool merchants passed through the customs house and their names were entered in the Port Book[2] as being the owners of a total of 1,600 goads of Manchester cottons which were due to be shipped to Bilbao in the *Michael* of Liverpool. But the entry was later crossed out, and a note in the margin informs the reader that 'these wares were not shipped forth, because the ship was pressed for the service of the Earl of Essex',[3] who happened to need it for an expedition to Ireland. What became of the cottons is not known, but they were certainly not shipped from Liverpool in any other vessel that year.

Useful Port Books have survived for several years after the war with Spain broke out. These books show that Liverpool's trade was reduced to a sorry state, having been so dependent on Spanish markets. In the first six months of 1585[4] no Manchester cottons were exported to the continent, although seven vessels left Liverpool bound for Ireland, each carrying pieces of Manchester cottons, making a total of 44 pieces. The shipping list which supplies this information does not give the measurements in goads, but the figure can be calculated to 968 goads.[5] By 1592[6] even this modest amount had dwindled to no more than seven pieces of cottons, and no exports of any sort were sent to the continent during that year. There was one noticeable difference from the 1585 exports: amounts of other types of cloth had begun to be taken to Ireland. Thirty-four Rochdale friezes, twelve other friezes, eight pieces of linen cloth called Manchester sackcloth, and four pieces of cloth described as coarse linen were sent to Ireland in 1592. At the end of the century almost all outward traffic from Liverpool had ceased. In 1600[7] no cottons were exported at

---

[1] E190, 1323/4.   [2] E190, 1324/4.

[3] Walter Devereux, first Earl of Essex (1541–76), who was attempting to subdue and colonise Antrim.

[4] T. Baines, *History of the Town and Commerce of Liverpool*, p. 242 passim.

[5] If these were full pieces they could be expected to be 33 yards or 22 goads long.

[6] E190, 1326/8.   [7] E190, 1327/30.

all and the only other cloth to be exported was eighteen pieces of Rochdale frieze and three kerseys worth £18 altogether, to Ireland.

Bristol seems to have played a similar sort of rôle to that of Liverpool in the export of Lancashire cloth, at least until the late seventies of the century. The first clear idea of the magnitude of Bristol's share in the trade is provided by the two Port Books for 1573/4,[1] which show that during that year 7,200 goads of Manchester cottons began their journey to the continent of Europe through Bristol, slightly fewer than the number which had passed through Liverpool the previous year. The Bristol exports were more or less equally divided between France and Spain, but there was one remarkable point—two new markets had appeared for the first time: the Canary Islands and Barbary. There were two separate consignments of Manchester cottons to the Canaries, both by Bristol merchants. The first was a large one of a thousand goads, aboard the *Speedwell* of Bristol, by Andrew Baker on January 27th. The second was in April when Thomas Dickenson despatched four hundred goads as well as some Reading kerseys. The Barbary shipment was entered in the Port Book under September 4th and was by John Porter, another Bristol merchant.

The scene was very similar two years later with Spain and France sharing the trade, and a single shipment of 200 goads to the Canary Islands by Miles Diconson, who sent along with his cottons, two pieces of Brecknock cloth and seventy northern kerseys.[2] The total amount of Manchester cottons exported through Bristol during that year, 1575/6, was 6,500 goads, slightly more than the Liverpool total for the same year.

Shortly after this, however, something went wrong; there was a sharp decline in the amounts of cloth handled at Bristol. In the year 1579/80 only 1,400 goads of Manchester cottons passed through the port, although even that was more than the year's exports of Welsh cottons which only achieved 500 goads.[3] In 1581/2 the figure for Manchester cottons had risen slightly to 1,800 goads, not very striking when one remembers that Liverpool was maintaining the level of her exports, the following year being one of her best for Manchester cottons. However, the Bristol exports of Welsh cottons were doing better than those of the Manchesters in 1581/2, having risen sharply to 2,800 goads.[4] After that in the sixteenth century, there was no distinction drawn in the Bristol Port Books between the various kinds of cottons, and the general level of exports seems to have been pretty low. In 1582/3 a total of 2,850 goads of cottons were exported from Bristol;[5] by 1598/9 the total was 1,700 goads of cottons;[6] but for these two years it is impossible to say how many were Welsh cottons and how many were from Lancashire. At the turn of the century there was an increase in cottons exports: in 1600/1 the amount reached 6,130 goads, but again

[1] E190, 1129/4 and 1129/6.   [2] E190, 1129/12.   [3] E190, 1130/2.
[4] E190, 1130/4.   [5] E190, 1130/5.   [6] E190, 1132/7.

the clerk failed to specify which were Welsh and which were Manchester cottons.[1]

This is as far as it is possible to go in the process of attempting to give accurate details about the export of Manchester cottons and other Lancashire cloth through London and the outports, and even these details leave much to be desired. One can say even less about the other ports which handled Lancashire cloth in the sixteenth century. Some was exported from Southampton, after being carried there by Manchester, Lancashire or Kendal pack-horsemen.[2] But how regular this trade was or how large the quantities of cottons involved were, is impossible to say, mainly because there is no distinction drawn in the Southampton Port Books between the different types of cottons. For instance, in 1583/4,[3] 500 goads of cottons left Southampton, 100 for Bordeaux, 200 for the Canary Islands, and 200 for St. Malo, which may or may not have been Manchester cottons. Similarly, it seems likely that some cottons were exported from Hull: certainly James Chetham, a Manchester clothier, sold cottons to a Hull merchant.[4]

Table 6. Exports of North of England cottons from English ports (in goads)

	London (Manchester and northern cottons combined)	Chester (Manchesters)	Liverpool (Manchesters)	Bristol (Manchesters)
1565/6		25,600 (£853)	6,900 (£230)	
1572/3			8,700 (£220)	
1573/4				7,200 (£240)
1575/6	70,174 (£2,340)* (half year)		5,600 (£187)	6,500 (£216)
1579/80				1,400 (£47)
1581/2				1,800 (£60)
1582/3		17,550 (£583)	7,000 (£233)	2,850 (all types of cottons)
1585/6			968 (£33)	(£97)
1592/3		110 (£3)	154 (£5)	
1594/5	73,611 (£2,453)			
1598/9	72,468 (£2,417)			1,700 (all types) (£57)
1600/1		147 (£5)	none	6,130 (all types)(£204)

* The London Port Books for 1576 (E190, 6/4) and 1598/9 (E190, 10/11) and the Bristol Port Books for 1753/4 (E190, 1129/4) and 1575/6 (E190, 1129/12) give, in many cases, the values of cottons exported. In all four books the values are remarkably similar, with no change at the end of the century. 1000 goads of Manchester or Northern cottons were usually worth £33 6s. 8d. Thus it was possible to calculate the approximate values of cottons exported, working to the nearest 100 goads.

---

[1] E190, 1132/12. [2] *supra*, p. 61. [3] E190, 816/4.
[4] *supra*, ch. iii. pp. 60–1.

To sum up then, it can be said that after a highly successful period in the middle years of the sixteenth century, exports of Lancashire woollens were definitely reduced, probably for ten years or so following the outbreak of war with Spain and the other hostilities on the continent of Europe. Chester and Liverpool, which had depended heavily on Spanish markets, ceased almost completely to export Lancashire cottons which had been almost the only type of Lancashire cloth which they exported, and neither of them seem to have recovered from this setback, at least during the sixteenth century. After 1585 there were some feeble attempts to switch the cottons exports to Ireland, but these seem to have petered out quite soon, at least as far as Chester and Liverpool were concerned, although Bristol continued to send cottons of some sort to Ireland. Both Liverpool and Chester did begin to export small quantities of friezes and coarse linen cloth to Ireland.

While the outports fared badly, London on the other hand appears to have recovered fairly quickly from the effects of the military disturbances, and exports of northern cottons and Manchester cottons combined had increased almost to the level of the 1570's, going almost exclusively to France. Northern cottons also held their own against their great Welsh rivals, and as the seventeenth century progressed, began to win control of the French markets.

There is some evidence to suggest that certain new types of cloth were introduced into Lancashire towards the end of the sixteenth century,[1] perhaps to offset the loss of markets for the old types of cloth, but what part they played in the export trade is obscure. The Port Books shed no light at all on the problem, but there is one glimmer of evidence to suggest that the Lancashire clothiers were staging a recovery, even before they began to produce real cotton goods. A list of woollen goods exported at the end of Elizabeth's reign mentions thirty thousand 'Lancaster newe devysed carsayes'.[2]

[1] *infra*, ch. vii.   [2] Hewart, op. cit., p. 25.

CHAPTER VI

GOVERNMENT REGULATION
AND CONTROL

DURING the Tudor period the government interfered continually in the country's textile industry. Its motives for doing so were mixed, so that it will be simpler to disentangle the various motives from each other and treat them separately. Some mention has already been made[1] of how the government attempted to bring down the price of wool by a Statute directed against the common wool broggers, forbidding the sale of wool except to Staplers or to cloth manufacturers.[2] But this was only one aspect of the government's aims. Another important motive was a desire to prevent the decay of the old corporate towns, out of which the cloth industry had begun to spread into the surrounding countryside. There is no one clear-cut reason for this spread of the industry outside the towns. At first the fulling mills left the town for the countryside in search of the water power which the new machinery required. Some people may have set up their looms outside the town boundaries in order to escape the restrictions of the town craft guilds; others may have felt that they could make a better living by combining their traditional agricultural activities with the manufacture of woollen cloth. But whatever the cause the result was the same: town industry began to decay and was faced with the competition of its rural rival. Wherever one looks in England it was the same story: towns such as York, Beverley, Coventry, Norwich and Bridgnorth were all losing ground and their industries decaying, while new towns and villages like Halifax, Leeds, Wakefield and Manchester were springing to the fore. As a result of this decay the towns themselves found it difficult to pay their annual farm to the Crown.

Bearing in mind this last fact above all others, the government determined to bolster up the decaying towns by preventing any further spread of the clothing industry into the nearby countryside. At the same time the government hoped that their measures would do something towards solving another serious problem, that of over-production, which had flooded the market during the 1540's and which was considered in many

[1] Ch. iii, pp. 21–3.   [2] 5 and 6 Edward VI, cap. 7.

quarters to have been largely responsible for the sudden depression in exports in 1551 and 1552, and for the depression of 1556, when all shipments of cloth to the Low Countries had to be delayed for four months, until the glut of cloth in that area should have time to ease off.[1] It is also worth noting again that the government's legislation against wool broggers might also be expected to restrain the spread of industrialisation and the subsequent over-production, by cutting off many small cloth producers from the source of their raw materials.

It was in 1555 that the government took the first step in its attempts at restraint. A statute[2] of that year, applying to Lancashire as well as to the rest of England, forbade the making of woollen cloth except in a city, corporate or market town, or in places where cloth had been made continually for the last ten years. No clothier outside such a town was to be allowed to keep more than one loom, and no weaver more than two looms.

Two years later, a second Act[3] laid down similar but more stringent regulations; cloth must not be manufactured outside a city, corporate or market town, except in places where it had been made for the last twenty years. As usual the Tudor government found such restrictive legislation difficult to enforce. It is generally accepted nowadays that these two statutes met with very little success anywhere in the country. As far as Lancashire was concerned, it is obvious from what has already been said that the Statutes were not applied very vigorously, to say the least. It is true that there were just a few presentments in the Courts of Exchequer and Queen's Bench, but they are very rare. In fact between 1560 and 1603, in the whole of Lancashire, only four men appeared in court for keeping more than the statutory allowance of looms.[4] Cloth manufacture was allowed to spread outside cities, corporate and market towns into the country districts around Manchester and the hills above Bury and Bolton. Lawrence Blakey, a clothier who lived at Blacko, well outside the boundaries of the market town of Colne, could own three looms without interference, in 1573, although it may be, of course, that cloth had been made by the Blakey family for the last twenty years.

The truth of the matter is that in so far as the legislation aimed to boost towns suffering from decay, it was hardly concerned with Lancashire at all, since there were very few corporate towns in the county. The main growth of the textile industry therefore lay outside such towns, so that Lancashire largely escaped the great struggle between urban guild interests and country interests which characterised the older clothing counties. The main centres of activity were the towns of Manchester, Bolton, Bury,

---

[1] *Acts of the Privy Council*, V, p. 295.
[2] 2 and 3 Philip and Mary, cap. 11.
[3] 4 and 5 Philip and Mary, cap. 5.
[4] M. R. Gay, 'Aspects of Elizabethan Apprenticeship', p. 143; in *Facts and Factors in Economic History: articles by former students of E. F. Gay*, Cambridge, Mass., 1932.

Rochdale, Blackburn and Colne, all of which were market towns, and might therefore have been expected to welcome those terms of the Statutes which aimed to prevent the textile industry spreading outside them. In fact, however, these towns, with the possible exception of Manchester, were very tiny. Rochdale, even in 1626, was little more than a few streets around the church and the market cross. Its buildings were mostly inns, woolshops, and warehouses of clothiers and drapers.[1] The great importance of these towns lay in their rôle as markets from which raw materials could be obtained and where the woven cloth could be taken for finishing and distribution, while the majority of the actual weaving took place in tiny hamlets on the surrounding hillsides. Of the ten owners of looms discovered in the Colne area, for instance, eight lived outside the town boundaries in the hamlets of Blacko, Wheathead-in-Pendle, and Winewall. The interests of the towns were so bound up with those of the surrounding countryside that there was no question of protection for the urban weavers against those of the country districts—it simply did not arise. The area enclosed by the boundaries of Manchester was much larger than those belonging to the other towns, so that a much larger proportion of loom owners in the Manchester area lived inside the town boundaries. But the same situation applied just as much there as elsewhere. The great Manchester clothiers who made a prosperous living buying and selling, and finishing cloth, relied just as much on weavers in the hamlets of Haughton, Heaton Norris, Barton, Eccles, Kearsley and Levenshulme, as they did on weavers operating in Deansgate. There can be no doubt that one explanation of the rapid rise in importance of Manchester cottons, and Lancashire rugs, friezes, linens and kerseys, lies in the near absence of corporate towns with their guild restrictions. Thus the industry was allowed to develop naturally and freely, with market town and surrounding rural areas working in harmony.

The vigorous growth of industry in and around Manchester and the other towns provides a striking contrast to the situations in Lancashire's two main corporate towns, Wigan and Preston, both of which tended to fall behind the rest during the sixteenth century, at least as far as woollen cloth was concerned. In 1571, white kerseys were being made at Preston[2] and some linen was produced there.[3] Yet in 1566 when the government appointed deputy aulnagers at every important centre of woollen manufacture, both Preston and Wigan had been ignored.[4] By 1702 the antiquary Thoresby could write of Preston that there were no merchants and no manufactures in the town which 'chiefly depended on the quill'.[5]

[1] Wadsworth and Mann, p. 55.
[2] D.L.1/83, L.6.   [3] D.L.1/62, B.17.
[4] 8 Elizabeth, cap. 12.
[5] W. A. Abram, *Memorials of the Preston Gilds*, p. 74.

The reason for this decay probably lies in the activities of the Preston Guild. Apparently the Guild Merchant and the corporation exercised their privileges very rigorously and selfishly and 'looked with jealousy on newcomers who might share their monopoly and diminish their profits'.[1] Their records contain cases in which very heavy entrance fees were charged to people who wanted to become burgesses, and the Court Leet imposed severe penalties on those who attempted to exercise any trade, without having been admitted. Even apprenticeship for seven years in the town was not sufficient, by itself, to give the right to carry on a trade without admission by Court Roll or at a Guild Merchant, coupled with the payment of the entrance fee.[2]

Liverpool provides an interesting examples of a weavers' guild in operation. In 1572 four Liverpool weavers received permission from the corporation to form a guild.[3] One of them was John Gore, a linen weaver. In 1577 another linen weaver, Miles Liptrott, was allowed to become a member of the guild.[4] Four years later Robert Ainsdale was fined for working as a weaver without being a member of the guild.[5] He was later allowed to join on payment of the sum of ten shillings.[6] The guild was still in existence in 1591 when a weaver named Robert Mawdesley became a member; he had to pay the considerable sum of twenty shillings, probably because he was not a native of the town, having moved in from Ormskirk.[7] At some date soon after this, the Liverpool weavers' guild may have become moribund, for there is no further mention of it in the Town Books. On the other hand, of course, there would be no need to mention it if no more weavers were admitted to its ranks. It must be remembered also that cloth manufacture was only a minor concern in Liverpool, the chief interest being in shipping.

One aspect of government attention which was probably not very successful in the long term, was its insistence in the Act of 1552[8] that all weavers should serve a seven-year apprenticeship. This obligation was extended in 1563[9] to include all persons exercising 'any Arte Mysterye or Manuell Occupation . . . nowe used or occupied within the Realme', which naturally included all kinds of clothworkers except spinners. Evidence shows that to some extent the legislation was being enforced. George Chetham and his younger brother Humphrey, who were destined to make fortunes from the cotton trade during the next century, both began their career in the traditional type industry. George was apprenticed for seven years in 1591, at the age of sixteen, to George Tipping, a Manchester linen draper. Humphrey also served his seven years, beginning

---

[1] W. H. Clemesha, *History of Preston in Amounderness*, p. 102.
[2] ibid., pp. 102–3.   [3] *Liverpool Town Books*, II, p. 26.
[4] ibid., p. 254.   [5] ibid., p. 384.   [6] ibid., p. 401.
[7] ibid., p. 602.   [8] 5 and 6 Edward VI, cap. 8.
[9] 5 Elizabeth, cap. 4.

in 1597, apprenticed to another linen draper.[1] At the Quarter Sessions of 1605 an apprentice was discharged from his 'apprentished', because he was bound contrary to the statute, 'viz for three years only'.[2] Between 1563 and 1603 there were twenty-four prosecutions in the Courts of Exchequer and Queen's Bench, which concerned weavers not apprenticed for the full seven-year term, and three prosecutions of weavers who had served no apprenticeship at all.[3] In 1581, for instance, two Manchester men, Francis Hough and Richard Morton, and George Holt of Salford, were prosecuted in the Court of Exchequer for 'occupying the art of clothworker and not being apprenticed to the same for the space of seven years'.[4] Three other Manchester men, John Leese, Adam Oldham, and Stephen Hulme, were prosecuted in the same court the following year for 'exercising and occupying the art of dyers', without having served the necessary apprenticeship.[5]

On the other hand, however, these prosecutions do not necessarily mean that the government's policy was effective. A prosecution did not always restrain a craftsman from continuing his occupation after the fuss had died down. What was to prevent him continuing as before once the fine had been paid? George Holt, for instance, continued his activities for another seventeen years, and died quite a wealthy man.[6] Francis Hough was not deterred from his weaving which continued to provide him with a very comfortable living until his death in 1593, twelve years later.[7] Two of the dyers, John Leese[8] and Adam Oldham, also continued their trade, and the latter was prosecuted again in 1583[9] and in 1584.[10] John Leese was still described as a dyer at the time of his death in 1598.

The final aspect of the government's interference in the cloth industry, and the one which it pursued with the greatest tenacity, sprung from its desire to impose regulations of standard sizes and weights on all cloth made in England. It is not surprising that since England's economy was so dependent on cloth exports, the government wished to ensure that this cloth was of the highest possible quality. Even before cloth exports became of paramount importance, there were the interests of the home customer to consider. As early as the reign of Edward I, a new office had been created, that of aulnager, who was to inspect and measure all cloths before they were offered for sale. The aulnager was to affix his own special seal to all satisfactory cloth, and for this service, the owner was expected to pay a small fee.

[1] F. R. Raines and C. W. Sutton, *Life of Humphrey Chetham*, p. 8.
[2] *Lancashire Quarter Sessions Records*, p. 256.
[3] Gay, op. cit., p. 143.
[4] E159/381, Mich. 23 Eliz. Rot. 108, 109.
[5] E159/382. Pasch. 24 Eliz. Rot. 81; and E159/385, Mich. 25 Eliz. Rot. 123.
[6] *supra*, ch. iii, pp. 31-3.   [7] *supra*, ch. iii. p. 34.
[8] *supra*, ch. iii, p. 36.
[9] E159/384, Pasch. 25 Eliz. Rot. 110.   [10] E195/386, Hill. 26 Eliz. Rot. 78.

The sixteenth century saw a continual struggle between the government and the cloth manufacturers and dealers. Numerous statutes appeared; the aulnagers were prodded periodically to ensure their vigilance; deputy aulnagers were appointed to make their job easier; there were sudden outbursts of judicial activity in which unfortunate clothiers found themselves answering charges brought against them by the local aulnager. Yet, as far as the Lancashire industry was concerned, for all its care and determination, it cannot be said that the government was any more successful in this than it was in other spheres of interference. Whatever immediate improvement might have been caused by each government effort, the effect was not lasting; at the end of the century exactly the same complaints and criticisms were being levelled at the whole English cloth industry as had been voiced in the early years of the century.

The first significant government action in its long struggle to achieve higher standards of cloth, occurred in 1514. The Tudor government, professing to be gravely disturbed at the poor quality of much of the English cloth being offered for sale, passed an Act for 'avoydyng decepts in making of Woollen Clothes'.[1] Regulations were laid down for spinners, weavers, fullers and clothiers, but any cloths made in Lancashire, Wales or Cheshire were to be exempted from the rules; at this early date in the century, the coarse northern cloth had not gained sufficient circulation to attract the government's attention. Twenty years later their attitude had changed, and Lancashire was included in the scope of the 1535 Act, 'for true making of Woollen Clothes'.[2] This specified that the clothier must put his own lead seal on each piece of cloth, which must then be inspected and sealed by the county aulnager. Any clothier selling cloth not properly sealed was to forfeit the cloth; half its value was to go to the Crown and the other half to the aulnager.

It is generally thought that the aulnage system was inefficient. In Wiltshire, for instance, the office had come to be chiefly fiscal rather than industrial.[3] In Lancashire the tale of relations between aulnager and manufacturer is long and complex. Some evidence suggests at first sight that in the Manchester area the aulnager made a genuine effort to enforce the statutes. In mid-century the aulnage of the county of Lancaster was in the hands of the Trafford family, and in 1545 William Trafford brought a case against two Manchester clothiers. Adam Scolcroft was one of them; he had sent away ten pieces of Manchester cottons. The other man, Henry Johnson, had sent away five pieces of rugs, all without a genuine seal. Both men had forged a seal, 'oon countre-fayte and vntrue Sealle'. Trafford had the cloth confiscated and claimed half of it for himself as was his legal right.[4]

---

[1] 6 Henry VIII, cap. 9.   [2] 27 Henry VIII, cap. 12.
[3] Ramsay, *The Wiltshire Woollen Industry in the Sixteenth and Seventeenth Centuries*, p. 53.
[4] *Pleadings and Depositions, Duchy Court of Lancaster*, ii, p. 209.

Two years later occurred another case in which the aulnager, now Margaret Trafford, William's widow, confiscated two packs of cottons which were being taken out of the county unsealed.[1] It may be, however, that there is more behind this evidence than meets the eye. It does not follow that because the aulnagers were seizing cloth, they were fulfilling their primary duty—to ensure that cloth was of the highest possible quality. In the second case the clothier concerned, Richard Crompton of Bury, appealed against the seizure of his cloth, and it emerged that he had actually paid his 4d., the fee for sealing two packs of cottons. However, the carrier had taken them away earlier than expected, with the result that the cloth had reached Stretford on its way to Chester, and was still unsealed. Although the aulnager's assistant was requested to examine and seal the cloth there and then at Stretford, he refused, and confiscated the cloth. The Court judged in favour of Crompton and the aulnager was ordered to compensate him.[2] The whole case casts a very doubtful reflection on the aulnager or his assistant. To begin with he had taken the fee for sealing without having seen the cloth he was supposed to have sealed. When he did eventually see the cloth, he confiscated it, without any legal right, because although he was perfectly justified in refusing to seal sub-standard cloth, ownership of inferior cloth was not in itself an offence. The aulnager was allowed to seize unsealed cloth only if the owner sold it or carried it out of the county, of which Crompton had done neither. Unfortunately any system which presents to the officials half the value of all confiscated goods, is bound to tempt the less scrupulous officials to seize goods at the slightest excuse, and even when no excuse existed.

An incident which occurred in 1550 shows up the system in an even less favourable light. Ralph Trafford, Margaret's son, began to act as aulnager illegally, without his mother's permission, and forged his own seal.[3] One of his servants, James Boardman,

by unlawful commandment of the said Rauf . . . accompanied by four riotous persons, came to the place where the said cloths were lying and riotously disturbed plaintiff's (Margaret Trafford) servants, and sealed the cloths with the forged seal, and took all the profits to his own use, and has ever since then used the office of aulnager and has sealed many cloths, not only in Manchester, but in diverse other places.

Ralph Trafford was evidently something of a doubtful character; he had previously been bound over to keep the peace towards his mother, and since then had behaved himself 'ungodly' . . . procuring 'sundry persons' to quarrel and brawl with his mother's servants.[4] It is rather too much to accept that this gentleman was inspired by a great desire to improve the

---

[1] ibid., iii, pp. 6–10.   [2] ibid., iii, p. 10.
[3] ibid., iii, pp. 95–7.   [4] ibid., iii, p. 95.

G

quality of cloth leaving Lancashire. Much more likely he was out to make a crafty shilling.

A sudden outburst of legislative activity on the part of the government about this time shows that the aulnagers' efforts, whether genuine or otherwise, had not prevented the circulation of faulty cloth. In 1550 appeared an Act[1] which is of great interest for the light it throws on the fraudulent practices still common in the cloth industry. It forbade excessive stretching or pressing of cloth, faulty dyeing, the use of flocks or inferior wool, and the use of chalk, flour and starch to make the cloth weigh heavier. It also specified—and this was a complete innovation— that in any town, village or hamlet, not incorporate, where any cloth was made or sold, the Justices of the Peace must appoint overseers to inspect at least four times a year, all premises where cloth was made.

Two years later appeared another Act,[2] in which Lancashire cloth was mentioned. This Act made similar complaints and prohibitions to the 1550 Act, and in addition, it specified the exact sizes and weights of almost every type of English cloth, including that made in Lancashire.[3] The aulnager's seal was not to be placed on any cloth which failed to conform to these standards.

Again it is quite clear that the new legislation met with no lasting success. It was the same story all over the country. The merchant interests at Blackwell Hall continued to be dissatisfied with the quality of cloth coming to London from the country districts. It was at their instigation, and especially at that of the Merchant Adventurers, that the City of London authorities, acting independently of the government, attempted to introduce a more effective inspection of cloth brought into Blackwell Hall for sale. If any cloth failed to measure up to the requirements of the statutes, the owners were to be fined.[4] Almost immediately in September 1561, sixteen Lancashire clothiers were fined for bringing defective cloth to the market. Five were from Manchester, three from Bolton, and one from Blackburn. The home town of the other seven men is not mentioned.[5]

Meanwhile the office of county aulnager had changed hands and now belonged to Thomas Leigh of High Leigh in Cheshire. He was to hold the office for twenty-one years from May 6th, 1561, at a yearly rent of 41s. 8d.

---

[1] 3 and 4 Edward VI, cap. 2.   [2] 5 and 6 Edward VI, cap. 6.
[3] *supra*, ch. i, 5.
[4] Ramsay, 'Distribution of the Cloth Industry in 1561–2', pp. 301–9. *E.H.R.*, LVII, 1942.
[5] ibid., pp. 302–9. The sixteen men were George Holland, Humphrey Houghton, John Davie, Edward Byddelstone and Adam Hill, all of Manchester; John Hendell of Blackburn; Edmund Chetham, John Howarth and Giles Ainsworth of Bolton; George Ainsworth, John Bucke, Edmund Taylor, Allen Hill, Thomas Tailor, James Ovenden and Adam Byram. Although Adam Hill's home town is not mentioned in the list, he was probably the man whose name appears in the *Manchester Court Leet Records*, i, pp. 90, 112, 133.

to the Crown.[1] In 1564 he brought a case in the Duchy Court[2] against four clothiers from Bolton and Bury who had carried unsealed cottons, friezes and rugs to London and elsewhere. He suggested that as well as this unsealed cloth, all their cloth still in Manchester should be confiscated. This seems to be a clear instance of the aulnager carrying out his duties. However, the defendants claimed that until the end of June 1562 either the aulnager or his deputies had always been on hand to seal cloths in 'at leaste foure of several market towns'. Since that date, however, the seal had been kept at one town only, probably Manchester, since the defendants were natives of Bolton and Bury. They claimed that this was most inconvenient for such as themselves and 'above nine hundreth poor householdes, havinge a greate parte of them living by the sayd trade and dwellinge distant from the towne where the sayd seal is kepte, eight to nineteen miles'. They accused Leigh of aiming to seal all cloth at Manchester for his own private gain; the result was that his deputies at Bolton and Bury refused to seal the defendants' cloth, whereupon they, 'being poor men', took the cottons to London unsealed, as many other clothiers did. In reply Thomas Leigh denied their charges and stated that his deputies had refused to seal the cloth because it was faulty. And in fact one of the defendants, John Howarth, had already been fined at Blackwell Hall in 1561 for attempting to sell faulty cloth.[3] Moreover their excuse that they could not afford the time to take their cloth to Manchester for sealing seems rather lame since they would probably have to pass through or near Manchester anyway on the journey to London.

Certain aspects of the case, however, show up the aulnager in an unfavourable light. At one stage Leigh, to give his case more weight and make the clothiers' guilt more apparent, admitted that they had been dealing in unsealed cloth for quite some time before they were prosecuted, and that during that time they had taken fifteen hundred pieces of cloth to London and other towns. All this unsealed and therefore possibly faulty cloth had been allowed to leave the county before Leigh made any move; by his own admission he seems to have been rather lax, to say the least. Why had he not acted earlier, the first time these clothiers broke the law?

Two years later Leigh was again active in court, this time against a man named Judd Ward of Salford,[4] whom he accused of forging a seal with which he sealed quantities of faulty cottons, rugs and friezes, which were later taken out of the county. In this case the defendant's reply seems reasonably plausible. His evidence contains allegations which suggest gross negligence on the part of the aulnager's deputies. It appears that the deputies were in the habit of selling the wax seals without inspecting any cloth whatsoever, to anyone who cared to pay the fees for

[1] D.L.1/83, L.6.
[2] D.L.1/60, L.4.
[3] *supra*, p. 88, footnote 5.
[4] D.L.1/68, L.3.

them. Men like Ward who bought seals from the deputies, were then at liberty to seal any cloth, faulty or not, provided the owners paid the fees. The seals used by Ward were, so he claimed, genuine ones supplied to him by the aulnager's deputies. If he was telling the truth, then it seems that clothiers could buy a stock of seals from a deputy, seal their own cloth and take it out of Lancashire without it being examined by the aulnager. The aulnage system in Manchester, Salford, Bolton and Bury at least appears thoroughly discredited, nothing more than a device for raising money. The deputies, with or without the approval of Thomas Leigh, were concerned only to collect fees, and not at all with the standard of the cloth. Unfortunately this is one of those frustrating cases where no record of the verdict has survived, and it is impossible to say with any certainty who was the guilty party. A nodding acquaintance with human nature would indicate that both sides were guilty to some extent, that is that the aulnagers did sell the seals, and that Judd Ward not unnaturally seized the opportunity to seal faulty cloth.

What is completely certain, however, is that faulty, poor quality cloth continued to leave the county: towards the end of the same year, 1566, the government felt it must deal specifically with the Lancashire industry. It passed an Act[1] introduced by an elaborate preamble which complained that many clothiers of Lancashire had recently carried cottons, rugs and friezes out the county without their being sealed by the aulnager, in order to 'cover and hyde the untrue and deceiptfull making of many of the sayd Clothes'. The Act demanded that before any cloth could be taken out of the county, both owner and aulnager should put their seal on it. The owner's seal was to have marked on it the length of the cloth when it was wet. The aulnager's seal was to bear the mark of a crowned portcullis on one side, and on the other, the weight of the cloth when it had dried out—the true weight of the cloth. If the aulnager or his deputies sealed any cloth without weighing it, they were to pay a penalty of twenty shillings for each pack illegally sealed. In addition, permanent deputy aulnagers were to be appointed in Manchester, Bury, Rochdale, Bolton and Blackburn. These men were instructed to affix the seal to the cloth personally, and not entrust the job to any assistant.

All this continual talk of 'untrue and deceiptfull making' of cloth might seem to suggest that Lancashire clothiers were a thoroughly dishonest bunch of characters who were out to defraud all and sundry. Yet if one looks more closely at them, it is obvious that some of the men who were accused of selling faulty cloth were among the most highly thought of and respected men in their town. John Davy, who was fined at Blackwell Hall in 1561, was elected boroughreeve of Manchester in 1567[2] and was one of the town constables in 1569.[3] Humphrey Houghton, also fined at

---

[1] 8 Elizabeth, cap. 12.
[2] *Manchester Court Leet Records*, i, p. 111.   [3] ibid., p. 127.

Blackwell Hall, held the position of boroughreeve a few years later in 1574,[1] positions hardly likely to be given to men who were considered to be slightly dishonest. It must be said in their defence that it was demanding too much of them to expect their cloth to conform exactly to the statutory requirements. It must have been most difficult for a clothier to judge exactly the size and weight of a cloth, because of the amount of shrinkage incurred in the fulling process, so that the cloth had to be stretched on tenterbars, back to its original size, as nearly as possible. In addition to this difficulty, clothiers had suffered a great deal from 'Crueltye of Informers and Searchers seeking continually their owne pryvate Gayne'.[2] The government showed itself to be well aware of the situation, and in the second part of the 1566 Act, tried to remedy their difficulties. All types of cloth were to be allowed to weigh rather lighter than the previous regulations had specified: cottons now twenty-one pounds, and rugs and friezes forty-three pounds. The length also was allowed to be very slightly less than before. But while the Act allowed these concessions, at the same time penalties for infringement of the rules were made more severe. For each pound lacking in weight, the clothier was to pay a fine of a shilling. But if a piece of cloth was more than three pounds light, the penalty was five shillings for each pound lacking beyond three. If a piece of cloth was longer than the specified length, the aulnager was warned to take care that the extra yards weighed the correct amount. For every goad or yard which failed to do so, the clothier was to pay one shilling.

In spite of these concessions, some clothiers still declined to have cloth sealed before taking it out of the county. In 1567, for instance, a Manchester clothier named John Houghton, took six packs of unsealed cloth out of the county, bound for Stourbridge Fair.[3] Unluckily for him the aulnager got wind of it, and as Houghton was passing through Bucklow Hill in Cheshire with a group of clothiers, the aulnager staged some sort of ambush and seized Houghton's cloth. Six other clothiers rallied round, helped Houghton to attack the aulnager, and rescued the six packs of cloth. After the excitement they all continued on their way to Stourbridge Fair. The result was another lawsuit, of which the verdict is not clear.

Leigh was especially active about this time and was involved in several other lawsuits. The corporation of Preston claimed that they alone should be responsible for sealing cloths in the town,[4] and that the county aulnager had no right to interfere. They refused to allow the deputy to operate, sealed all the cloth themselves, and kept the fees. Justifying this behaviour in court, the mayor of Preston, William Banester, quoted a charter dating back to the reign of Henry III, which allowed the burgesses to be free of any interference by the aulnager. The mayor also claimed that most of the cloth made in Preston was narrow white kerseys, and since no mention

[1] ibid., p. 165.
[2] 8 Elizabeth, cap. 12.
[3] D.L.1/87, L.1.
[4] D.L.1/83, L.6.

of this type of cloth was made in any Statute concerning aulnage, Thomas Leigh had no legal right to interfere. In this case the aulnager was victorious and obtained a Court Order to the effect that the corporation must pay him the duties, 'notwithstanding the charter'.[1]

Two other cases,[2] in 1573 and 1574, involved two groups of Colne clothiers, who were accused by the aulnager of taking large quantities of unsealed cloth into Yorkshire. The Colne men, however, produced an excellent answer. The cloth which they had taken into Yorkshire consisted of raw kerseys, which had not been fulled, shorn or dressed. The aulnager's seal could not very well be fixed to these cloths, they claimed, because if they were fulled with the seal on them, 'by the violence and force of the fullinge mill whiche dothe knocke the same peces together, woulde be made full of holes and therebye the clothe marred and destroyed utterlye'. The argument was also put forward that immediately after weaving it was impossible to know what the final length, breadth and weight of a piece of cloth would be, because it would be shorter and lighter after being fulled and dressed. They had been forced to take these pieces to Heptonstall in Yorkshire because that was the nearest place where they could have them properly fulled; apparently there were no good fulling mills in Colne.[3] The Colne clothiers went on to say that after their cloth had been fulled and dressed at Heptonstall, it was then inspected and sealed by the Yorkshire aulnager, to whom they paid the required fees. They had in no way broken the law, they claimed, because the Statute applied only to finished cottons, rugs, and friezes, whereas their cloth consisted solely of raw kerseys. This seems a reasonable enough argument, and again the impression is that the aulnager cared more about his own loss of profit to the Yorkshire aulnager, than about the quality of the cloth concerned.

One might have expected that such activity on the part of the aulnager would lead to at least some improvement in the quality of Lancashire cloth. But apparently it did not. In 1577 John Leake produced his famous treatise on the cloth industry.[4] He complained that a great deal of 'false cloth' was being made in England and the chief cause of it was 'want of execution of oure good lawes and bearing too much with thoffender; whearin I will not onlie accuse the Clothier, but those that shoulde see to it'. Thus Leake's reference to the aulnagers is distinctly critical. Significantly he made a special condemnation of the 'Northe partes, wher', he lamented, 'no true clothes are made'. Northern cloths, he said, were worst of all for poor dyeing, shortness of weight, and excessive stretching.

Even the deputy aulnager for Manchester who had only the one town to look after, was unable to cope with the problem and so in 1591, for the

---

[1] *Historical Manuscripts Commission, 14th Report*, p. 601.
[2] D.L.1/83, L.6.   [3] *supra*, ch. iii, p. 88.
[4] Printed in Tawney and Power, op. cit., iii, pp. 210–25.

first time, the Court Leet appointed an officer to assist him—'a mesure for Clothe, bothe of wollen and lynen'.[1]

At the end of the century the Elizabethan government made a last determined effort to improve the standards of Northern cloth, along with that of the rest of the country. The Statute of 1597[2] attributed most of the trouble to the excessive use of tenters for stretching the cloth, and it completely forbade the use of any such machine at any stage during cloth manufacture. This was impossible to enforce, since no cloth could be put on the market unless it had been stretched back into shape after its immersion in water during the fulling process. Thus there were violent protests from the Lancashire Justices of the Peace, in deference to which, in January 1601, the Privy Council authorised the retention of tenter bars.[3] This was the gist of their reply:

> Wee have received your letters . . . wherein you thincke it not convenyent the tenters should be plucked down and defaced, though by the Acte of Parlyament the same is expresly ordayned, . . . although wee see no reason but that which by statute was then appointed should be performed, yet in regard of the reasons alledged by . . . so many gentlemen of calling in that countie . . . we thincke convenyent . . . first, that the lower barr of the tenters sturr not neither up nor down, so as they maie not be removed after the clothe is sett on them nor the clothe streyned by any kynde of meanes. Secondly, we thincke meet . . . that . . . all suche as do tenter clothes . . . maie be sworne . . . that they shall not strayne nor stretche any clothe.

For all the difference this made to the difficulties of the clothiers, the Privy Council might just as well have saved their time and paper. What earthly use were tenterbars if they were not to be moved and the cloth still not stretched? Appreciating this point to the full, the Manchester Justices, when they made the order for this amendment to be carried out in April 1601, ignored the latter part of the Privy Council's order and permitted some stretching of the breadth of the cloth, up to three inches.[4] Nor do they seem to have attempted to enforce the Statute rigidly: there is not a single case at the Quarter Sessions of any clothier accused of illegal stretching of cloth, for over two years.

Between January and May of 1601, however, the complaints about the poor quality of English cloth, especially from France, where Henry IV had recently confiscated large amounts of cloth which was claimed to be defective, led the Privy Council to revoke their January order. In May a letter to the Justices of Lancashire and several other counties utterly forbade the use of all tenters, to stretch either the length or breadth of the cloth.[5] 'All ropes, headdes and lower barres, etc., which are or may

---

[1] *Manchester Court Leet Records*, ii, p. 56.   [2] 39 Elizabeth, cap. 20.
[3] *Acts of the Privy Council*, xxxi, pp. 78–9.
[4] *Lancashire Quarter Sessions Records*, p. 97.
[5] *Acts of the Privy Council*, p. 388.

be used for stretching', were to be removed. The Preston Justices of the Peace immediately issued an order that 'the lower bar of all tenters shall be taken away by the owners thereof and the overseers already appointed, within 14 days next'.[1] An Act of October 1601 extended these conditions to the whole country.[2]

It seemed as though the local Justices meant business, and soon afterwards, a man appeared at the Preston Quarter Sessions on a charge connected with the Act. He was John Hargreaves of Barrowford in Pendle, near Colne, and the charge was that he 'took out the pins outside his tenters and so allowed the lower bar to go at large, contrary to the order of the overseers'.[3] This, however, was the only case of illegal tentering at Preston Sessions in 1601, and there were no cases at all during the next two years. At the other Lancashire Quarter Sessions—Manchester, Ormskirk and Lancaster—there were no immediate presentments; and yet tentering must have gone on; it was essential that it did. It looks as though the Justices simply turned a blind eye to the practice, except for the one gesture at Preston.

Then in May of 1603 the Manchester Justices suddenly bestirred themselves for the first time, after ignoring the law for exactly two years, and four men appeared in Court, charged with illegally stretching pieces of cloth on a tenter with a lower bar. Jeremy Wolstencroft of Middleton, one of the offenders, 'also assaulted John Fitton and James Hopwood, the overseers in this matter', and rescued his piece of cloth.[4] After this brief outburst of activity the efforts of the Justices subsided, and there were no other cases of this nature, at least during the next three years.

There can be no doubt that although the Justices and overseers were honest and probably genuinely desired to secure some conformity to the statutes, they faced tremendous difficulties. The Statutes had gone too far, were too severe in their restrictions, and were therefore impossible to enforce. Moreover the whole industrial organisation was so complex that it would have taken a great army of overseers all working full time to eliminate all defective cloth. The job was really quite beyond the part-time overseers. Evidently the Justices were content to let matters slide, with an occasional outburst of prosecutions to keep up appearances.

What was needed to cope with the situation was some entirely new institutional system of control. This fact was recognised by the Royal Commission which was appointed to investigate the problem and which published a report in 1640.[5] The report began by bewailing all the deceitful practices still used in the manufacture of cloth. It went on to propose

---

[1] *Lancashire Quarter Sessions Records*, p. 104.
[2] 43 Elizabeth, cap. 10.
[3] *Lancashire Quarter Sessions Records*, p. 106.   [4] ibid., p. 172.
[5] 'Report of the Royal Commission on the Clothing Industry, 1640.' Printed in *E.H.R.*, LVII, 1942, pp. 485–3.

that a completely new organisation should be set up, which would be centrally controlled. It would take the responsibility out of the hands of the Justices, and would extend to all the worst offending towns in England. It is significant that among the list of towns to be treated in this way were Manchester, Rochdale, Bolton and Bury.

CHAPTER VII

THE CHANGING SCENE AT THE
TURN OF THE CENTURY

DURING the last fifteen years of the sixteenth century, the Lancashire textile industry was in a state of flux. Overseas markets had been interfered with almost continuously from 1585 until the end of the century, although the interruptions in trade were not always of the same seriousness. The most troublesome crisis was that lasting from 1586 to 1588,[1] and another serious slump occurred in the late 1590's,[2] both of which affected the Dutch and German markets. The Manchester clothiers mentioned earlier,[3] were just three of the many who must have encountered great difficulty in selling friezes and rugs, and also cottons, since the Spanish market for cottons was completely inaccessible for the last fifteen years of the century.

It seems only reasonable to suppose that these disturbances must have had some effect on the outlook of Lancashire clothiers. The uncertainty of the markets was bound to make them think about some sort of readjustment, if they were to survive. There would probably be satisfactory years for cloth exports, yet clothiers could never be sure what the next year might bring, so long as there was the prospect of hostilities in the Netherlands and at sea. With typical northern determination, Lancashire clothiers seem to have reacted swiftly and switched to the production of other types of cloth. If not as much cloth could be exported, then they must produce a cloth which would be acceptable to people at home. They achieved this in several ways.

In the first place, they began to manufacture a new type of cottons, which were very similar to the older type of cottons in every respect save colour: they were grey instead of the highly coloured varieties which had been produced earlier. These new grey cottons were suitable for the home market. The Lancashire clothiers soon came into conflict with the London aulnagers, who thought that the new cloths were friezes, and therefore wrongly sealed. In 1595 the clothiers replied to these charges in a docu-

---

[1] *supra*, ch. v, pp. 66–8.   [2] Gould, op. cit., p. 221.
[3] *supra*, ch. v, p. 67.

ment[1] which explains the situation exactly. They claimed that only the colour of the cloth was different, 'which cullour was lately devised for the greate good of the countrey and releive of the poore therein'. They had been compelled to manufacture them, they said, because the wars had destroyed the trade in the old cottons.

The trade of the oulde sorte of cottones which were sent into France, Spayne, and other places, was cleane overthrowne, by reason of warres and trobelles that happened in those countryes where they were usuallie vented and soulde, so that these graye colloured cottones (beinge fitt for England) were putt in use and made, to the great good of many peopell and releive of greate nombers of familyes and howseholdes in the countrey, which otherwise had [been] given to greate wante and misery yf the cullour had not bene altered and devized, as nowe yt ys used.

Actually there was a difference in finish as well as in colour. Shearmen were to be allowed eightpence for the 'well rowinge and burlinge of every peece . . . in respect they neyther shere them nor cotton them as they doo other cottons fitting for forraine trade beyonde the seas and elsewhere'.

As often happened in such documents, there seems to be some exaggeration here: it was not exactly true for instance, to claim that the overseas markets for cottons had been 'cleane overthrowne'—the export figures for 1594/5 and for 1598/9 show that quite clearly.[2] However, this does not alter the main fact that not as many traditional northern cottons could be exported, and so some clothiers changed over to producing the new type of grey cottons for the home market. This may well explain why the 1598/9 London exports of northern cottons remained lower than those of Welsh cottons,[3] even though the French markets were accessible. Lancashire clothiers were simply not producing as much of the old type of cottons for the time being, having found satisfactory markets at home for the new cottons. Later they probably drifted back to traditional cottons, as the overseas markets improved permanently, and in due course captured the French market from the Welsh.

The second way in which Lancashire clothiers attempted to readjust their activities, was by turning to the production of linen cloth instead of woollens. It has already been suggested that the linen industry, well fed with raw materials from Ireland, underwent some expansion towards the end of the sixteenth century.[4] This fact must be emphasised: the sudden blossoming of the linen industry producing cloth mostly for home consumption, was probably a direct result of the contraction of the overseas markets for woollens. The wills examined show that before 1585 there was a fairly even distribution of workers between the woollen and linen

[1] Wadsworth and Mann, p. 12.
[2] *supra*, ch. v, p. 69.   [3] *supra*, ch. v, p. 69.
[4] *supra*, ch. iv, p. 54.

industries. The change after 1585 is quite remarkable, especially in the Manchester area. In all, the wills of thirty-seven people occupied in some field of the textile industry in and around Manchester, and who died after 1585, have been found. Twenty-six were concerned with linen; four were merchants and dealt with both linens and woollens, and only seven out of the thirty-seven were occupied exclusively with woollens; four of these seven had had a lot of trouble selling their cloth either in London or at Stourbridge Fair.

After all, it should not have been too difficult for a woollen weaver to adapt his loom so that it could produce linen cloth, or for a clothier with a little capital behind him to experiment with dealings in linen yarn. This would explain why Lawrence Robinson who, from all the signs in his will and inventory, had been chiefly concerned with woollens, had bought three large packs of linen yarn shortly before his death in 1587, perhaps hoping in this way to offset what he seemed likely to lose on the cloth he had been unable to sell in London.[1]

Another fact which bears out this impression of both small-scale and prosperous workers being driven out of the woollen industry is the number of linen weavers who owned sheep enough to provide them with a basic supply of wool should they have chosen to produce woollen cloth; yet they ignored this possibility and manufactured linen instead. John Derbeshire of Eccles was one of them: he owned sheep worth £4, which must have numbered between thirty and sixty,[2] and he had some wool worth £1 6s. 8d. in his house. But his main concern was with linen cloth, for which he had raw materials valued at £10. A similar case is provided by Thomas Pollitt, another Eccles husbandman, who died in 1588, leaving sheep worth £2 and wool worth 12s. But again, his household was geared to the production of linen, and his linen yarn and cloth were valued at £17. However, the boom in the linen industry probably did not last much beyond the turn of the century, for by 1602/3 imports of linen yarn through Liverpool had fallen almost to the pre-war level.[3]

Two centres of woollen production do not seem to have changed to linen. These were Rochdale and Colne which continued to produce woollens and which, in some ways, were more closely akin to the West Riding of Yorkshire than to Lancashire; neither of them had ever had much to do with cottons. Colne continued to produce kerseys; and another possible reason for the lack of change in Rochdale was the fact that by 1592, Rochdale friezes were finding an outlet to Ireland.[4]

At the end of the sixteenth century, other new cloths had appeared on the scene and some were beginning to play a significant part in the export trade. These were the so-called 'Lancaster newe devyzed carsayes' which were mentioned in a list of woollen goods exported at the end of Elizabeth's

[1] *supra*, ch. iii, p. 41.
[2] See Appendix B, p. 101.
[3] E190, 1328/2.
[4] E190, 1326/8.

reign.[1] Apparently thirty thousand of these were exported during the year, but their nature is rather mysterious. Exactly what was new about these kerseys is difficult to say, but the ordinary type of kersey was nothing new in Lancashire, having been produced in Colne and Preston for years.

The most momentous innovation of all in the second half of the sixteenth century was the introduction of the cotton industry, which first appeared in the form of fustians, a combination of cotton and flax, and later developed into the production of pure cotton cloth. This fustian manufacture may well have begun on a small scale in Lancashire as early as the 1560's, for already at that time small quantities of fustians were being exported to Ireland from Chester. In 1565/6 for instance, two pieces of fustian went to Ireland.[2] In 1576/7 the figure was four pieces,[3] while in 1584/5, a half piece of fustian was sent to Ireland.[4] Since large quantities of Manchester woollen 'cottons' were exported from Chester, it is not too much to assume that these fustians had been made in Lancashire. Yet until the end of the sixteenth century, the extent of fustian manufacture must have remained small. Not until 1601 is there any mention in surviving records of a fustian weaver; in that year a fustian weaver named George Arnold was working in Bolton.[5] In 1600/1 twenty-two pieces of fustian were exported to Ireland from Chester.[6]

The new cotton, the 'Bombast or Downe',[7] was also used in a second combination with flax or linen yarn in production of the cloth known as checks, which was apparently 'linen and cotton mixed and striped for men's and women's wearing'.[8] They also began to play a part in the export trade, for in 1602/3 eight dozen of these cloths, described as Manchester checks, were sent to Ireland from Chester.[9]

From these small and tentative beginnings developed the vast industry which was destined to change the whole scope and organisation of the Lancashire textile scene. This growth is a subject which has of course, been exhaustively investigated by Wadsworth and Mann, and it would therefore be superfluous to repeat what they have already written. However, it is worth remarking briefly how the organisation of the new industry differed from that of the old. It has been described how, in the older woollen and linen industries, the clothworkers were largely independent, although towards the end of the century there were some threats to their independence. From the very beginning the same was never quite

[1] Hewart, op. cit., p. 25.
[2] E190, 1323/1 and E190, 1323/10.
[3] E190, 1324/17.
[4] E190, 1325/15.
[5] *Lancashire Quarter Sessions Records*, p. 121.
[6] E190, 1327/28.
[7] Cotton wool was so described in 1621 by the London fustian dealers in a petition to Parliament. Quoted by Wadsworth and Mann, p. 15.
[8] ibid., p. 116.
[9] E190, 1328/20. This is a long time before the earliest reference to checks quoted by Wadsworth and Mann, which was about 1699.

true of the cotton industry. The important factor of difference was that supplies of cotton were limited and intermittent and could only be obtained from London. This meant that the cotton and fustian dealer stood in an extremely strong position towards the producer to whom he gave credit for his purchase of raw materials and whose goods he bought.[1]

Eventually, as the volume of trade grew, the dependence of producer on dealer became uncomfortably close, and some producers were heavily in debt. In the first twenty years of the seventeenth century, however, the capitalist fustian and cotton dealers had not quite gained a monopoly of the industry. There was still a certain amount of freedom of markets, with the existence of weekly markets for fustians, such as the one at Bolton which was frequented by numerous yarn dealers and buyers of cloth.[2]

During the same period, and probably until about the 1680's, the organisation of the older woollen and linen industries remained much more loose, as it had been during the previous century. This was because supplies of raw materials were less restricted and the market for woollens and linens was wider. Thus woollen and linen weavers continued to obtain raw materials from one dealer and to dispose of their products to another.[3]

As the seventeenth century wore on, whereas the older industries remained loosely organised, the organisation of the cotton industry became even more rigid than it had been at first. By the last two decades of the century, the open market for fustians had almost disappeared, before various forms of the putting-out system, thus marking the end of the independent producer.[4]

It was at about the same time that the woollen industry began to change and to lose its free organisation. Apparently woollen manufacturers began to go over to the production of worsteds.[5] This changeover was a fairly chancy business at first, and some capital and risk were necessary to overcome the initial difficulties.[6] The result was that the woollen industry too became capitalistic, and many spinners and weavers were reduced to the position of dependent employees. But this is rushing on far into the future. At the end of the period covered by this study, not many people could have foreseen the great changes that were to take place during the next century, for in 1600 the cotton industry was still taking root and the breakdown of the 'independent producer system' was only just getting under way.

[1] Wadsworth and Mann, p. 36.   [2] ibid., p. 38.
[3] ibid., pp. 39, 46, 47.   [4] ibid., p. 80.
[5] ibid., p. 87.   [6] ibid. ,p. 88.

APPENDIX

A. *A note about sheep*

Most of the inventories at Preston which include sheep, mention only their total value and not the exact number of animals. However, a few inventories do mention the number of sheep as well as the total value, and from these, it is possible to get some idea of the numbers of sheep involved in the other inventories, even though the values accorded to the sheep vary considerably.

The following table includes all the sheepowners discovered whose inventories mention the number of sheep involved:

Name	*Date*	*No. of sheep*	*Value*			*Approx. value/sheep*
Alexander Parker, Colne	1574	24	£1	13s.	4d.	1s. 5d.
Nicholas Baldwin, Colne	1587	60	£6			2s.
Alice Hardman, Barton	1588	5		11s.	0d.	2s. 2d.
Thomas Pollitt, Eccles	1588	17	£2			2s. 4d.
John Abbott, Blackburn	1597	24	£3	6s.	8d.	2s. 9d.
John Hardman, Bury	1581	77	£11			2s. 10d.

Thus it can be calculated, admittedly rather roughly, that Lawrence Blakey of Colne, who died in 1573, leaving sheep worth £11, may have owned as many as a hundred and fifty sheep, if one assumes that they were of similar quality to Alexander Parker's animals. On the other hand, if Blakey's sheep were a better variety, or if they were still to be sheared, they may have numbered only about seventy-five.

B. *A note about looms*

The majority of inventories left by Lancashire weavers and clothiers mention 'pairs' of looms. At first I assumed, not unnaturally, that this meant two looms. Later on, however, when I found the inventory of George Holt of Salford, 1598, which mentions three pairs of looms, I began to doubt whether any sixteenth-century Lancashire clothier would have owned a house or a work-house large enough to accommodate six looms, which after all, must have taken up a fair amount of space.

It was obviously important to determine what exactly was meant by this word 'pair', since it could be significant in showing how capitalistically organised the Lancashire textile industry had become by the end of the sixteenth century. If George Holt owned six looms, he could almost be regarded as a budding factory owner.

The values given for looms in the inventories shed no light whatsoever on the problem, because they vary so widely. However, one piece of evidence pointed to the fact that Lancashire clothiers often talked of looms in the plural when they really meant only one loom. This is the inventory of John Abbott, a Blackburn yeoman farmer and clothier, who died in 1597. The document mentions 'a woollen piece in the looms'.

   This impression was borne out by Mr. Wilfred Spencer, formerly the Librarian of the Colne Public Library and now Librarian of the Nelson and Colne College of Further Education. He very kindly drew my attention to a reference in Wright's *English Dialect Dictionary*, which confirms that 'a pair o' looms' means one loom. The dictionary gives as its source *A Glossary of Rochdale-with-Rossendale Words and Phrases*, compiled by H. Cunliffe, and published in 1886.

C. *Inventories*

Following, in chronological order, are the inventories of six men, each representative of a different group of workers in the textile industry. I have omitted the words 'inprimis' and 'item', replaced the Roman numerals with Arabic numerals (except in the case of George Holt, where Arabic numerals were used), and substituted the modern £ sign for 'li', normally used in sixteenth-century inventories.

(1) JOHN NABBS of Manchester, a woollen weaver described in his will as a clothmaker. The will and inventory are dated 1570 (see p. 29).

An inventory of the goodes and cattels of John nabbs in tyme of his lyffe prysed by 4 dyscret and honest men whose namys herafter folowe

	Olyver Byrche hughe shaclocke	Mylys gylfort John cowhope
too kye		53s. 4d.
in heye		26s. 8d.
in fuell as turvis wood and cols		20s.
on fourms paneal		10s.
in olde barrels		2s.
4 pannys 6 potts and on posnet	£3	
15 pewter dyssys and 7 sossers 2 trenkets 2 salts a pewter kann a pewter bolle and a pewter bassen		12s. 6d.
on brasyn morter 2 chandelers a chafynge dyshe a skellet a brasyn ladyll and 3 spytts		9s. 8d.
frying pan and dryppyng pan and a greddyll and a skeymer 2 brendderth and a payre of tonnkes and rackenteth and pothokes at		7s.
5 stonds and 2 keres and a chourne at		6s.
3 esshyns 3 bassyns 2 tree[n?]chargers 2 toungs and a knedyng tournell and 3 pyggens and a salting bauke		5s.
2 bordes 2 fourmys 2 cheres 4 stoulys 6 quyssyns at		6s.
3 pare of stocke kards 4 pare hande kards and on lomme at		11s. 8d.
a sherebord and handels		2s. 8d.
in cloth to his backe		40s.
redy money		40s.
5 matresses 5 coverletts 9 pare of shets 11 blankets & boulsters & pylloys		£3 5s. 8d.
in bedstoks and coufers and arks		20s.
on olde hangyng		12d.

4 bord nabkens	4 grots
3 emty barrels	16d.
on lead	6s. 8d.
on lytyll cofer and a trest	16d.
on borde cloth and a towell	2s.
21 hopys of corne	35s.
in spinnyng whellys	20d.
in treane and paynted clothys	11s.
19 peses of cloth at	£25
9 score stone and 4 of wolle and flockes	£36
in dettes	£5
	Septem 1570

(Total £89 19s. 6d. not given)

(2) ROBERT BIRCH, a prosperous Manchester linen draper. The will and inventory are dated 1582/3, (see pp. 53–5).

A true Inventory of all the goodes and cattalls of Robert Berche late of Manchester in the County of Lancaster Lynnyne Draper deceassed. Taken the 11th day of Marche Anno Domini 1582.

1 packe of whyte yarne	£25
80 poundes of fyne white yarne	£8
60 and 14 poundes of whyte yarne	£4 6s. 8d.
100 poundes of whyt yarne	£5 8s. 4d.
100 poundes of whit yarne	£5
20 poundes of whit yarne	30s.
20 poundes of whit yarne	25s.
5 poundes of cullard yarne	7s. 6d.
100 poundes of gray yarne	£5
93 poundes of gray yarne	38s. 4d.
6 poundes of gray yarne	4s.
16 poundes of whit yarne	16s.
5 poundes of Irishe blought yarne	5s.
3 poundes of gray yarne	2s. 6d.
11 poundes and a half of bytten yarne	4s. 8d.
12 poundes of gray yarne	9s.
5 poundes of gray yarne	15d.
18 poundes of Toe flaxe	4s. 6d.
4 brode peses	£7 12s.
10 brode peses	£17 10s.
15 brode peses	£24
3 brode peses	£4 10s.
in gray yarne	£6 12s. 7d.
3 quarter of a pounde of cullard yarne	15d.
20 peses of sackclothe	£19
20 peses of sackclothe	£17
6 peses of sackclothe	£4
3 bolster peses	50s.
506 poundes of flaxe	£9 5s.
5 Chandlers and 1 salte	8s. 8d.
4 Cannes 1 potte and 1 salte	6s. 4d.
3 floware pottes	12d.
37 poundes of pewter of London mettall	24s. 8d.

H

19 poundes of Wiggen mettall	9s.	6d.
4 trenkettes		20d.
1 standinge bed 1 trucle bed 2 Mattes 2 cordes	20s.	
3 fleaches 3 bordes 1 twiggen basket in the chamber	2s.	6d.
2 Scales and half a beame		12d.
21 poundes and a half of lead weightes	2s.	8d.
2 stoane and 12 poundes of feathers	11s.	6d.
2 kyne and a heffer	£4 10s.	
5 jagges and a half of course hay	23s.	
3 ketle ponnes	9s.	
28 poundes of ponne mettall	14s.	
1 brasse potte of 10 poundes weight	3s.	4d.
1 Skellet and a fryinge panne		20d.
2 spyttes and 2 hacking knyves		16d.
1 gridle 2 golbardes a paire tongues an yron barre	4s.	
3 base bordes a throe and a hennpenne	2s.	
an yron. a pair of pothookes and lynkes of yron and a candlesticke of yron	6s.	
in Fuell	3s.	
2 paire of Lomes and a Reale	13s.	4d.
5 stoundes and 1 bouttinge tubbe	2s.	6d.
1 Eshynne. 2 runges. 3 piggens. 4 bassons a dishecrate. dishes and potliddes	4s.	6d.
bordes in the Buttry	3s.	4d.
a longe table. a Cubborde 6 buffet stoles and seelinge 3 chayres and and 1 Ratchmonde	£2 13s.	4d.
a short table	3s.	4d.
in painted cloathes	3s.	4d.
a round borde and 2 stoles		12d.
a paire of gold weightes		8d.
a bible	12s.	
a standing bed and a truckle bed	18s.	
Curtaines and fringe	14s.	
a feather bed. a Mattresse 2 blanchetes and a caddowe a paire of sheetes a bolster and a pillowe lyinge on the standinge bed	40s.	
a mattresse. a caddowe 3 coverlittes 2 blanketes a paire of sheetes a bolster and a pillowe lyinge on the trucle bede	23s.	
1 Caddowe 1 bolster and 1 pillowe	11s.	
5 cushons	3s.	4d.
a carpette	5s.	
a truckle bed		16d.
a paire of sheetes and 4 pillowe bears of flaxen	18s.	
5 sheetes of a corser sort	14s.	
a dosson of dioper napkins	4s.	
4 napkins		12d.
a Syve cloathe and a bord napkin	2s.	8d.
3 table cloathes	4s.	
a forme and a coffer	2s.	
in his apparell	£5 10s.	
a Nagge	26s.	8d.
a Saddle bridle and gurthes	5s.	
a skonnce		3d.
2 sylver sponnes	8s.	
3 poundes of yarne	2s.	

a callivar	5s.
in glasse and a casmonde	4s.
in greene ginger	18d.
in ready money and gould	£96 13s. 4d.
Debtes owinge to the deceased as appeareth by byls and his booke	

(Then follows a list of about 130 debts owing to Birch, totalling just over £270. However, the list gives only the names and amounts owing, and does not say what the debts were for. Total value of goods, not including debts, is not given, but is £302 6s. 10d.).

(3) JOHN CLEGG or CLEDGE, of Newbold near Rochdale, who carded and spun wool. The will is dated 1587 (see p. 26).

Inventory of the goods of John Cledge Late of newbalde

3 kyne	£5
the hey	30s.
in wolle and yorn	£15 15s.
in beddinge and bestockes	50s.
3 arkes	10s.
3 bushell of meale	30s.
in brasse	£3
in pewter	5s.
in wodde wessell	5s.
his apparell	20s.
spyninge wheles comes cardes and chears with all other implementes within the house	10s.

Smā £31

Prysed by Robert whitworth
Edwarde scolfilde william sale
and Otywell hill

(4) JOHN HEY of Eccles, a successful linen weaver. The will is dated 1597. (see p. 47).

This is a true Inventorie of all the goodes & Cattelles of John heye of the Boothes Late Deceassed prysed by these persons whose names bee here under wrytten That is to saye John Cheydocke, Henrye Cowpe, Gyles Dunster and Richard Smethurste.

three kyne and a litle Calf	£7
in whyt yarne bothe Flaxen and Canves	£9 13s. 4d.
in Beddinge wollin and Bolsters	42s.
in Sheetes and all other Lynnen	26s. 8d.
in Brasse	42s.
in Pewter	14s.
his Lomes heldes and Reades	14s.
in haye	30s.
in Turves Coles and kennell	20s.
one litle Arcke and four Coffers	15s.
4 payre of Bedstockes	7s.
stonndes and all treene vessell	13s.
one Almarie	4s.

one dishe bord and all other bordes	10s.	
all the iron ware	5s.	
in Butter and Cheese	19s.	
all his apparell shapen for his bodie	£4	
a tacke of grounde of mr. Thurstan tildisley	£10	

Summa totalis £43 15s.

(5) EDWARD BUTTERWORTH of Rochdale, a poor woollen weaver. The will and inventory are dated 1598 (see p. 27).

A true Inventorie of all the goodes and Chattells of Edward butterworth of Collin hey late deceased as Followeth viz. 1598.

three kyne the price is	£6		
one bay Mare with her furniture belonginge therto		40s.	
in hay and strawe		26s.	8d.
in woll and Clothe	£4	10s.	
in Meale and groates		40s.	
in beddinge	£3	6s.	8d.
in his Apparell		13s.	4d.
in Chistes		20s.	
in bedstocks		3s.	4d.
in Flaxe		6s.	8d.
in brasse and pewter		33s.	8d.
in woodden vessell		4s.	
one paire of loomes		3s.	4d.
in wheeles with Coomes and Cardes and Combestockes		4s.	8d.
one harrow, one spade, one shoole with an Axe and a mattocke		4s.	
one Rackontree with Tonges with a paire of Cilps and all other Implementes		2s.	6d.

Sūma total £23 18s. 10d.

prysed this 24th day of
November by

⎧ Raphe butterworthe
⎪ James Collenge
⎨ Cuthbert butterworth
⎪ & Cuthbert scholfeld
⎩ do show

(6) GEORGE HOLT, a prosperous Salford woollen clothier. The will and inventory are dated 1598 (see pp. 31–3).

A trewe and perfect Inventory of all the goods and Chattelles belonginge to George Houlte of Salford decessed taken and praysed the Thirteenthe of June Anno domini 1598 . . .   . . . by Rauffe Byram Thomas Byram James Glover and Hughe Pendleton as followeth.

In the myddle Chamber

a payre of Creeles a payre of warping woues a stock a troughe two fleckes 4 trestes a Ladder a wiskett and a Barrell	5s.	
one Beame and payre of scales		12d.

In the further Chamber

one standing Bedd	£1	6s.	8d.
one seeled Chist		4s.	6d.

one Troockle bedd		4s.	
2 Presses	£1	13s.	4d.
one great seeled Chist		8s.	
one other great Chist		5s.	
one Foulden Table		6s.	8d.
one little Squared Table		3s.	
2 Flocke Beddes		10s.	
2 Fether Bedes one boulster and 2 Pyllowes	£2		
2 white blanckettes		10s.	
3 Coverlettes		13s.	4d.
One payre of sheetes		4s.	
one New Covering	£2		
2 Fustian Pyllowes		5s.	
5 Whitte Blanckettes	£1	5s.	od.
one Canvis sheete		2s.	
waighed 8 stonn and a half of White Irishe woll at 4s. 4d.	£ 1	16s.	10d.
waighed 3 stonn and a halffe of a nother sorte of white Irish woll at			
3s. 4d.		11s.	8d.
more 4 stonn and a half of Englishe woll at 6s. a stoun	£1	7s.	od.
26 stonn and a halffe of grey Irishe woll at 3s. 4d.	£4	8s.	4d.
23 stonn and a half of dyed black woll at 3s. 4d.	£3	18s.	4d.
10 stonn and 4 pound of blacke Irishe woll at 3s. 4d.	£1	14s.	2d.
6 stonn of Flockes at 2s. 4d.		14s.	
5 stonn and 12 pounde of greye warpped woll and wefte at			
3s. 8d.	£1	1s.	9d.
16 stonn and a haffle of fyne warpe at 6s. 8d.	£5	10s.	od.
14 stonn and a half of white warpe at 5s.	£3	12s.	6d.
9 stonn of greye and Reeld warpe at 4s. 4d.	£1	19s.	od.
5 stonne and a half Fyne wefte woll at 8s.	£2	4s.	od.
one stonne and 4 pound of blew woll at 6s.		7s.	6d.
5 stonne and 12 pound of fyne warpe wolle at 4s. 8d.	£1	6s.	10d.
9 stonn of Fine white woll at 12s. a stonn	£5	8s.	od.
12 pound of Redd sellviche and woll at 6s. a stonn		4s.	6d.
one hand Baskett			6d.
one Madd wheele		1s.	
4 yeardes double Twill		2s.	
one white Pettycote a penone(?)		4s.	
one ould Chist			8d.
one oulde womans Saddle and a Brydle		6s.	8d.
28 pound of Tallow at 4d. a pound		9s.	4d.
Hay Cannell		1s.	
in ould Iron lockes and certayne Tooles		2s.	6d.
one payre of Fyne Flaxen sheetes		10s.	
one other payre of Flaxen sheetes		8s.	
6 payre of fyne Canvis sheetes	£1	10s.	od.
2 pyllow beares wth a blacke lace		8s	
one other pillow beare with a Jayed lace			
other pyllow Beares	(values illegible)		
. . . Boardclothe 3 yardes			
siffe Clothe			
one Table Napkin wrought with Blacke		1s.	
2 white Table Napkins		1s.	

In the Cabin

the Bedd with the Furniture	18s.

In the New Chamber

10 hoopes of Barly at 5s.	£2	10s.	0d.
4 hoopes of Ote meale at 5s.	£1		
2 hoope of grotes		7s.	
one Meale Arke		3s.	
one sifting Tubb and a kneding troughe		1s.	
one Brewing keyre		3s.	
2 Barrells		2s.	6d.
2 Runges		1s.	2d.
3 sives			6d.
one little Barrell with grease in			4d.
one secke 2 pokes		1s.	4d.
9 Cheeses		9s.	
one Board and other peeses of Tymber			8d.
2 Joystes		1s.	4d.
4 table Feete 4 Rackes one flecke and 2 trestes 3 borde endes and a payre of weyes		4s.	6d.

In the house

one Cupbord	£2		
one Longe Table and six stooles	£1	6s.	8d.
one shorte Table		5s.	
one glasse Case and 4 glasses and a Pott		2s.	
one holbert		3s.	
one seeled Cheare		3s.	
one throne Cheare		1s.	
3 pleane Cheares and littell Cheare		1s.	
one salt Chist		1s.	8d.
6 greene Quishions		4s.	
3 Sett quishens		6s.	
2 Carpettes		8s.	
one Byble		16s.	
one Brushe			4d.
one payre of Bellows			3d.
one Iron Chymny		6s.	8d.
one Bread Iron			3d.
2 payre of Tonges			7d.
2 payre of Potthockes and 3 Rakentythes		1s.	6d.
the paynted Clothes about the howse		1s.	
a hanginge Towell and the Cupbord Clothe		1s.	
Salt			8d.
Nyne score and twelve pounds of Pewter at 7d. a pound	£5	5s.	0d.
7 Chandlers		14s.	8d.
2 Chaffron dishes		2s.	6d.
a morter and a Pestle		1s.	
2 dripping pannes		4s.	6d.
one Brasse Morter and a Pestle		8s.	
one Ladle and Skymmer			8d.
one Frying Pann			4d.
one Fleshe sooke a backspitle a hackinge kniffe and a shreading knife			10d.

one grydd Iron			4d.
2 skellettes			8d.
4 hang pannes waing 56 pounds at 6d. a pound	£1	8s.	od.
4 other Pannes wainge 98 pound at 6d. a pound	£2	9s.	od.
in Pott Mettall 79 pound at 5d. a pound	£1	16s.	3d.
in Iron Ware 28 pound at 2d. a pound		5s.	10d.
one Brundreth 17 pounds at 2d. a pound		2s.	10d.
one little fyer Iron		2s.	

In the Parlor

one standinge bedd and a trucle Bedd	£1	8s.	od.
one Presse		10s.	
2 greate Chistes		12s.	
2 Mattrisses		6s.	
one Fether bed a Bolster and 2 pillowes	£1		
2 Blanckettes		5s.	
2 Coverlettes		12s.	
one payre of sheetes		4s.	
one Boulster		2s.	
2 ould Blanckettes		2s.	
one ould Covlett		2s.	6d.
one New Coverlett		5s.	
one other ould Blonckett		1s.	
2 yardes of Broade Clothe	£1		
one New Cloke	£2	4s.	od.
one Blacke Cloke		5s.	
one other oulde Cloke		3s.	
one shipe Coller Jerkyn		2s.	6d.
one Fryse Jerkin		1s.	4d.
one shippe Coller hose with moules		2s.	6d.
one payre of Kersey hose		2s.	
2 dooblettes		2s.	6d.
one payre of stockinges and a payre of shewes		2s.	
one hatt		1s.	
a payre of garters			2d.
4 bandes		3s.	4d.
3 shirtes		5s.	
a Sword and dagger		5s.	
a knitt Capp			4d.
a payre of Bootes spurres and Boote hose		4s.	
a Caunse			4d.
a Wiskett			4d.
a Blacke bill and a sallett		2s.	6d.
a hedging Bill a Pikeforte a wokinge staffe		4s.	
6 Towells and an oulde Clothe		1s.	4d.
one doble kerchiffe		2s.	
2 new doble kerchiffes		2s.	
2 single kerchiffes			6d.
a silke hatt		3s.	
in oulde Iron			6d.
2 spades one shovell a Mattacke or necessary tooles for husbandry		13s.	4d.
4 ould quishions			6d.
one Flaxen Borde Clothe 3 yardes		2s.	5d.
2 Canves ones		1s.	4d.

a Flaxen Towell		4d.
one Beeffe Turnell	6s.	
Salt beefe	6s.	
3 beare Barrells	4s.	
5 standes	5s.	
3 butter Tubbes	1s.	
one Costrell and a Cann		8d.
one Eshin		10d.
3 Mugge Pottes	1s.	
4 Runges	1s.	
16 milke Bassens	3s.	
one Broade Charger		6d.
3 Cheesefortes		8d.
2 pitche Cannes		6d.
one dossen meate Trenchers		2d.
one dossen Case Trenches		6d.
one milke Cupbord	2s.	6d.
2 drininge Pottes		4d.
a bagbreade and a Cheese ladder		4d.

In the Servantes parlor

one Bedd with the Furniture	6s.	8d.
a Backstonn and a board		8d.
one Cupbord	10s.	
2 Eshens		8d.
the Dishcrate with dishes Noggins and sithe	1s.	
9 Pyggins	2s.	
on Chorne and Staffe	1s.	
one greate keyre	1s.	6d.
one greate stonnd	2s.	
Earthen Pottes Pitcher		8d.
a payre of waies a sott Py[1] a Dessen a wiskett	1s.	
an ould Runge hackinge Bordes a stoole	3s.	
one greate Borde	2s.	6d.
all the Boardes and shelves about the kytchin		8d.
a wheele bedd frame	1s.	
a Fornace with the Curbe	£1	

In the Workehowse

3 payre of Loomes	10s.	
3 wheeles	1s.	4d.
3 payre of stocke Cardes	6s.	
more in wiskettes	1s.	
3 payre of handcardes		6d.

In the Backside

the Swyne and Troughe	18s.	
in Coales	2s.	
8 oulde Barrells and two Eshens	3s.	
a stonne Troughe a grindleston	2s.	
a Trest		4d.
a Jgg[2] for Ragges	1s.	6d.

[1] The letters in this item are perfectly clear: unfortunately their meaning is not.
[2] Again the letters are clear but the meaning is obscure.

all the Fyer wood about the howse		5s.	
a Leade for Treyne	£2	10s.	0d.
2 Joystes and 8 base bordes		2s.	6d.
8 Cloven peeses of wood			6d.
the Sadle Brydle and the Moe		3s.	4d.
4 Cratches a horse Combe and a Manger		1s.	
a hen penn			8d.
a gang of spoakes		2s.	
ould Barrell with fethers in		3s.	

In the Garden

one hyve of Bees		6s.	8d.
a gryndlestonn and a Cheese stonn		1s.	
in Donge		2s.	
2 little yates and a Ladder			4d.

In the ware howse myll and Country

37 Fryses at 27s. a Pesse	£46	19s.	0d
one white Rogge	£1	10s.	0d
22 Rugges at 21s. a pese	£23	2s.	0d
a standing bedd	£1	10s.	0d
Pack Clothes and Cordes	£1		
the Base Bordes aboute the Ware howse		4s.	
the bordes aboute the Warehouse		3s.	4d.
a Powle an Ashler		2s.	6d.

In the Barne

in Straw and haye	2s.	
2 Powes 2 pesses of wood and a Packe		6d.

In Babbcliffes

one Blacke Cowe	£3		
2 other Cowes	£6		
a nother Browne Cow	£3		
a geldinge	£4	13s.	4d.
an Acre of Otes	£3		
halffe an Acre of Barley	£2	10s.	0d.
the grasse	£1	10s.	0d.
owing by John Gandy		14s.	
in Sheepe at moberleye	£1	16s.	0d.
more Sheepe at Rbte Bolton		15s.	

In money Plate and debtes

in money		2s.	
one silver salte doble gylt 11 ounces at 6s. an ounce	£3	6s.	0d.
one Silver Cann parcelles gilte 18 ounces at 5s. 4d.	£4	16s.	0d.
one Tunne and a Goblet 18 ounces at 5s. ounce	£4	10s.	0d.
19 silver spoones wayed six ounces & a halfe at 4s. 8d.	£6	3s.	8d.
4 ounces Pinnes and hookes at 4s. 6d.		18s.	
one Bill dew from Thomas Bright	£10		
one Bill dew by Henry Bright	£14		
one Bill dew by Dennyell Dyckonson	£6	8s.	0d.
one bill by Raphe Morris	£20		
one Bill Charles Royle	£3	17s.	0d.

H*

one Byll by Richard Dennys	£3	16s.	8d.
one Byll by Henry Torkington	£5	2s.	6d.
The Revercon of one Bill of James Romsbothom		6s.	
owinge by Ann Blackshaw	£27		
by John Mosse of Cambridg	£7		
Thomas Bradshaw Carryer		9s.	6d.
Edward Wild		3s.	6d.
Richard Clegg		4s.	3d.
Gilbart Marshall		11s.	
Katheryn Syddall and her husband owethe me		8s.	2d.
Jone Lomas		1s.	
James Powell		3s.	
Hamlet Gilbody		3s.	
Nycholas Leese		5s.	
Ftten		6s.	6d.
Cycely Rothewell		2s.	
Katheryn Rosterne		1s.	
Arthur wieffe moades		1s.	6d.
Arthur Hobkyn		9s.	
Alyce Powne		18s.	
Willm Smith		18s.	
Willm Bradshaw for the hier of a Cow and for lent money	£10	4s.	0d.
in woll		4s.	
more woll		3s.	4d.
vi doossen of handells 2 crates one shere bord		4s.	5d.
2 Flores containinge 20 Joystes 2 F ... and Fortye ... Bordes (part of this entry is illegible)	£1		
Raphe Byram Thomas Byrom			
James Glover ...			
(the rest of this entry is illegible but the total value of all the items in the inventory can be made out)	£329		

GLOSSARY

almarie: a cupboard.

ashler: a square hewn stone for building purposes or for pavement.

brandereth, brendreth: a gridiron.

caddowe: a rough woollen bed covering.

caliver, callivar: a light musket or harquebus, introduced in the sixteenth century.

cannel, kennell: a bituminous coal which burns with a very bright flame.

casmonde, casement: a window frame.

caunse: some sort of flat stone; a flagstone.

costrell: a vessel for holding wine or other liquids, with an ear by which it could be suspended from the waist.

cratch: a rack to hold fodder for horses and cattle.

eshin, esshyn: a wooden pail or shallow tub.

golbarde, gaubert: the iron rack in a chimney that supports the pot-hooks.

jagge, jag: a load (of hay).

kere, keyre, kier: a large vat in which cloth is boiled for bleaching or other purposes.

piggin, piggen: a small vessel for drinking out of or a small wooden pail for milking.

posnet: a small metal pot or vessel having a handle and three feet.

rakenteth: a chain.

ratchmonde, ratchment: part of a wooden framework?

sallet: some kind of iron vessel.

sconce, skonce: a lantern or candlestick with a handle and a screen to protect the light from the wind.

skillet, skellet: a metal cooking pot with three or four feet and a long handle.

yate: a gate.

BIBLIOGRAPHY

1. PRIMARY SOURCES

(a) *Manuscripts*

At the Lancashire County Record Office, Preston:
   Unbound wills and inventories.
At the Public Record Office:
   C.1. Early Chancery Proceedings.
   D.L.1. Duchy Court of Lancaster Pleadings.
   E.159. Exchequer, King's Remembrancer, Memoranda Rolls.
   E.190. Exchequer, King's Remembrancer, Port Books.
   Req. 2. Requests Proceedings.
   S.P.12. State Papers, Domestic, Elizabeth I.

(b) *Printed*

Acts of the Privy Council, 1542–1628, ed. J. R. Dasent and others (1890–1940).
Axon, E. A. (ed.). *Documents Relating to the Plague in Manchester (Chetham Miscellanies,*
   Chetham Society, New Series, vol. 73, 1915).
Calendar of State Papers, Spanish.
Chippindall, W. H. (ed.). *A Survey and Year's Account of the Estates of Hornby Castle,*
   Lancashire (Chetham Society, New Series, vol. 102, 1939).
Dennett, J. (ed.). *Beverley Borough Records* (Yorkshire Archaeological Society;
   Record Series, 84, Wakefield, 1933).
Earwaker, J. P. (ed.). *Court Leet Records of the Manor of Manchester,* vols. i and ii,
   1552–1618. Manchester, 1884.
Farrer, W. (ed.). *Court Rolls of the Honour of Clitheroe,* 3 vols. Manchester, 1897,
   1912, 1913.
Fishwick, H. (ed.). *Pleadings and Depositions, Duchy Court of Lancaster,* 3 vols.
   (Lancashire and Cheshire Record Society, vols. 32, 1896; 35, 1897; and
   40, 1899).
Grosart, A. B. (ed.). *Towneley Hall MSS: The Spending of the Money of Robert Nowell*
   of Reade Hall, Lancashire. Manchester, 1877.
Hardy, W. J. (ed.). *Historical Manuscripts Commission: Kenyon MSS.* London, 1894.
Harland, J. (ed.). *Court Leet Records of the Manor of Manchester, 1586–1612* (Chetham
   Society, vol. LXV, 1865).
Harland, J. (ed.). *Shuttleworth House and Farm Accounts,* 4 vols. (Chetham Society,
   vols. XXXV, XLI, XLIII, and XLVI, 1856–8).
House of Commons Journals.
Report of the Royal Commission on the Clothing Industry, 1640. Printed in *English*
   Historical Review, vol. LVII, 1942.
Statutes of the Realm (1810).

Tait, J. (ed.). *Lancashire Quarter Sessions Records* (Chetham Society, New Series, vol. 77, 1917).

Twemlow, J. A. (ed.). *Liverpool Town Books*, 2 vols. Liverpool, 1918 and 1935.

2. CONTEMPORARY ACCOUNTS

Camden, W. *Britannia*, ed. E. Gibson, 2 vols. London, 1695.

Leake, J. *Treatise on the Cloth Industry*, 1577. Quoted by R. H. Tawney and E. Power, *Tudor Economic Documents*, vol. iii, pp. 210–24. London, 1924.

Leland, J. *Itinerary*, 1535. ed. L. T. Smith, 5 vols. London, 1906–10.

Hitchcock, R. *Pollitique Platt for the development of fisheries*, 1580. Quoted by Tawney and Power, *Tudor Economic Documents*, vol. iii, pp. 239–56.

3. MODERN WORKS

Abram, W. A. *Memorials of the Preston Gilds*. Preston, 1882.

Aston, J. *Manchester Guide*. Manchester, 1804.

Axon, E. A. *Chetham Genealogies* (Chetham Society, New Series, vol. 50, 1903).

Baines, T. *History of the Town and Commerce of Liverpool*. London, 1852.

Bennett, W. *History of Burnley*, 4 vols. Burnley, 1946–51.—*History of Marsden and Nelson*. Nelson, 1957.

Bowden, P. J. *The Wool Trade in Tudor and Stuart England*. London, 1962.

Bowman, W. M. *England in Ashton-under-Lyne*. Ashton-under-Lyne, 1960.

Bridgeman, G. T. O. *History of the Church and Manor of Wigan*, vol. i (Chetham Society, New Series, vol. 15, 1888).

Clemesha, H. W. *History of Preston in Amounderness*. Manchester, 1912.

Croston, J. *History of the Ancient Hall of Samlesbury*. Manchester, 1871.

Daniels, G. W. *The Early English Cotton Industry*. Manchester, 1920.

Fishwick, H. *The History of the Parish of Lytham* (Chetham Society, New Series, vol. 60, 1907)—*The History of the Parish of Poulton-le-Fylde* (Chetham Society, vol. 8, 1885)—*The History of Preston in Amounderness*. Rochdale, 1900—*The History of Rochdale in the County of Lancaster*. Rochdale, 1889—*History of the Parish of St. Michael's-on-Wyre* (Chetham Society, New Series, vol. 25, 1891).

Friis, A. *Alderman Cockayne's Project*. Copenhagen and London, 1927.

Gay, M. R. 'Aspects of Elizabethan Apprenticeship.' In *Facts and Factors in Economic History: articles by former students* of E. F. Gay, Cambridge, Mass., 1932.

Heaton, H. *The Yorkshire Woollen and Worsted Industry*. Oxford, 1920.

Hollingworth, R. *Mancuniensis*. Manchester, 1839.

Longfield, A. K. *Anglo-Irish Trade in the Sixteenth Century*. London, 1929.

Mendenhall, T. C. *The Shrewsbury Drapers and the Welsh Wool Trade in the XVI and XVII Centuries*. London, 1953.

Morris, R. H. *Chester in the Plantagenet and Tudor Reigns*. Chester, 1893.

Raines, F. R. and Sutton, C. W. *Life of Humphrey Chetham*, 2 vols. (Chetham Society, New Series, vols. 49 and 50, 1903).

Ramsay, G. D. *The Wiltshire Woollen Industry in the Sixteenth and Seventeenth Centuries*. Oxford, 1943.

Rowse, A. L. *The England of Elizabeth*. London, 1951.

Tupling, G. H. *The Economic History of Rossendale*. Manchester, 1927.

Ure, A. *The Cotton Manufacture of Great Britain Investigated and Illustrated*, vol. i, London, 1836.

Victoria County History of Lancaster.
Wadsworth, A. P. *History of the Rochdale Woollen Trade.* Rochdale, 1925.
Wadsworth, A. P. and Mann, J. de L. *The Cotton Trade and Industrial Lancashire.* Manchester, 1931, reprinted, 1965.
Willan, T. S. *The Early History of the Russia Company, 1553–1603.* Manchester, 1956.
Woodward, D. M. *The Trade of Elizabethan Chester.* University of Hull. Occasional Papers in Economic and Social History. No. 4 (1970).   .

4. ARTICLES

Bagley, J. J. 'Matthew Markland, a Wigan mercer; the Manufacture and Sale of Lancashire Textiles in the Reigns of Elizabeth I and James I' (*Lancashire and Cheshire Antiquarian Society*, vol. LXVIII, 1958).
Gould, J. D. 'The Crisis in the Export Trade, 1586–1587' (*English Historical Review*, vol. LXXI, 1956).
Hewart, B. 'The Cloth Trade in the North of England in the Sixteenth and Seventeenth Centuries' (*Economic Journal*, vol. 10, 1900).
Jones, B. C. 'Westmorland Packhorsemen in Southampton' (*Cumberland and Westmorland Antiquarian and Archaeological Society*, vol. LIX, 1960).
Ramsay, G. D. 'The Distribution of the Cloth Industry in 1561–1562' (*English Historical Review*, vol. LVII, 1942).
Willan, T. S. 'Trade Between England and Russia in the Second Half of the Sixteenth Century' (*English Historical Review*, vol. LXIII, 1948).

INDEX

Abbott, John, 35
Abbott, William, 35
Accrington, 1, 22, 57
Agriculture allied with textile industry,
    Ch. III and Ch. IV
Allofield, William, 39
Amsterdam, 70
Antwerp, 66, 70
Apprenticeship: cases of clothiers not
    legally apprenticed, 33; dyers not
    legally apprenticed, 36; apprentice-
    ship of clothworkers for seven years
    required by Statute, 84–5
Ashton-under-Lyne, 17, 52, 60
Aulnage system, Ch. VI, 85f., 96–7
Awen, William, 56

Baguley, William, 38–9, 40
Baldwin, Nicholas, 8
Bamford, Thomas, 45
Banbury, 58
Banester, William, 3, 91
Barbary, 78
Baron, Thomas, 8
Barrowford, 94
Barton-on-Irwell, 10, 40, 83
Bayonne, 66, 70
Bedford, 58
Beverley, 59, 81
Bilbao, 70, 75–7
Billington, 47
Birch, Robert, 53f., 103–5
Birch, William, 54
Birkenshaw, Robert, 23
Biscay, 70, 75
Blackburn, 1, 4, 5, 8, 28, 35, 43, 47, 50,
    57, 60, 61, 75, 83, 88, 90; linen
    manufacture at, 45; importance of
    cloth manufacture at, 58
Blackledge, Robert, 7

Blackley, 50
Blacko-in-Pendle, 35, 82
Blackstone Edge, 1, 3
Blackwell Hall, 59f., 67, 88
Blakey, Lawrence, 8, 35, 82, 101
Bleaching of linen yarn, 44f., 47
Bolton, 1, 3, 5, 9, 43, 60, 61, 82, 88, 90,
    95, 99, 100
Bolton, William, 8
Bordeaux, 66, 70, 76, 79
Boulsworth Moor, 1, 38
Bowyer, Simon, 24
Bradshaw, James, 50
Brerewood, Robert, 16, 17
Bridgnorth, 81
Bristol, 11, 59; exports of Lancashire
    cloth from, 78–9
Brownsword, Thomas, 49
Broxopp, John, 5, 28
Bucklow Hill, 91
Burnley, 1, 3, 4, 7, 9, 21, 43, 57, 59;
    fulling mill at, 3; importance of cloth
    manufacture at, 58
Burscough, 58
Bury, 1, 3, 5, 9, 40, 41, 61, 82, 87, 90,
    95; fullers at, 37–8
Bury St. Edmunds, 53, 58
Butterworth, Edward, 27, 106

Calais, 66, 70
Cambridge: as market for Lancashire
    woollens, 32; as market for Lan-
    cashire linens, 52
Camden, William, 2–4
Canary Islands, 78–9
Carding, 25f.
Chadwick, Nicholas, 28
Checks, 99
Chester, 2, 11, 21, 40, 59, 61, 63, 76;
    linen yarn and wool imports from

Map of Lancashire showing places
mentioned in the text

LANCASTER

Bowland
Rimington
Downham
Blacko · Foulridge
CLITHEROE
Roughlee · COLNE
Barrowford
Winewall · Trawden
St Michaels on Wyre
Bradley · Gt.Marsden
Poulton le Fylde
Pendle
Hill
Whalley
Gawthorpe Hall
Padiham · Ightenhill
Gt.Harwood · BURNLEY
Habergham
Rishton · Towneley Hall
Church · Clayton le Moors
PRESTON · Samlesbury
BLACKBURN · ACCRINGTON
Heptonstall
Lytham
Halifax
R. RIBBLE
Hoole
Haslingden

Chorley
Stoneyheys
Adlington
ROCHDALE
Burscough
Blackrod
Tottington · BURY · Newbold
ORMSKIRK
BOLTON
WIGAN
Radcliffe
Middleton
Bickerstaffe
Kearsley
Heaton Park · OLDHAM
Prestwich
Moston
Booths
Eccles
SALFORD · MANCHESTER
ASHTON
Barton
UNDER
Rusholme · Hulme
LYNE
Stretford
Levenshulme
Chorlton
LIVERPOOL

R. MERSEY
Warrington

R. DEE

CHESTER

WJS

0   5   10   15   20
MILES